W9-CDV-087

"A superb volume! Nicoletto offers keen new explorations of the Scriptures of the lectionary, illuminating them through lenses at once cosmological, scientific and poetic, and inviting readers into new avenues of spiritual growth and wisdom. An invaluable treasure trove for preachers and all who ponder the Scriptures!"

— Mary E. McGann, RSCJ
        Adj. Associate Professor of Liturgical Studies
        Jesuit School of Theology and Graduate Theological Union
        Berkeley, California

Journey of Faith, Journey of the Universe

The Lectionary and the New Cosmology

Ivan Nicoletto, OSB Cam

LITURGICAL PRESS
Collegeville, Minnesota

www.litpress.org

Cover design by Monica Bokinskie. Images courtesy of Thinkstock.

The following poems are reprinted with permission: Rebecca del Rio, "Constant"; Barbara Deming, "Spirit of Love," in *We Are All Part of One Another: A Barbara Deming Reader*, ed. Jane Meyerding; Galway Kinnell, "Astonishment"; Mary Oliver, "First Happenings," in *New and Selected Poems*; Bernard Schlager, "How About a Prayer for All Marriages (And All Committed Relationships Rooted in Love)?"; Julie Cadwallader Staub, "Measurement."

William Stafford, "The Way It Is," from *Ask Me: 100 Essential Poems*. Copyright © 1998, 2014 by the Estate of William Stafford. Reprinted with the permission of The Permissions Company, Inc. on behalf of Graywolf Press, Minneapolis, Minnesota, www.graywolfpress.org.

Scripture texts in this work are taken from the *New Revised Standard Version Bible: Catholic Edition* © 1989, 1993, Division of Christian Education of the National Council of the Churches of Christ in the United States of America. Used by permission. All rights reserved.

© 2015 by Order of Saint Benedict, Collegeville, Minnesota. All rights reserved. No part of this book may be reproduced in any form, by print, microfilm, microfiche, mechanical recording, photocopying, translation, or by any other means, known or yet unknown, for any purpose except brief quotations in reviews, without the previous written permission of Liturgical Press, Saint John's Abbey, PO Box 7500, Collegeville, Minnesota 56321-7500. Printed in the United States of America.

1   2   3   4   5   6   7   8   9

Library of Congress Cataloging-in-Publication Data

Nicoletto, Ivan.
    Journey of faith, journey of the universe : the lectionary and the new cosmology / Ivan Nicoletto, OSB Cam.
        pages   cm
    Includes bibliographical references.
    ISBN 978-0-8146-4825-4 — ISBN 978-0-8146-4774-5 (ebook)
      1. Church year meditations.   2. Nature—Religious aspects—Christianity—Meditations.   3. Biblical cosmology—Meditations.   I. Title.

BX2170.C55N53   2015
242'.3—dc23
                                                        2015015775

Contents

Year C

Foreword

One of the challenges of the liturgical readings from Scripture is for them to stay fresh—that is, for us, hearing them many times in a lifetime, to continue to listen to them deeply. We may, subconsciously, feel we know them and have little left to learn. An opposite situation arises from the discourse around the so-called new cosmology, where the language and concepts may seem so strange—even forbidding—to us that we can't find a way in. The very unfamiliarity of the science and philosophy, the geology and physics, may close our ears to what is offered there for us.

Journey of Faith, Journey of the Universe, by Ivan Nicoletto, OSB Cam, provides wonderful assistance for each of those challenges. He knows the Scriptures intimately, from both a lifetime of study and the liturgical home in which all the Benedictine traditions live. And he has steeped himself in the world of cosmogenesis, studying with the recognized experts in the field, becoming deft at making the complexities of that new discourse accessible for lay listeners. The reflections provided here integrate these two realms in ways that are both insightful about Scripture and illuminating about the cosmogenesis viewpoint: one of the signs of the times in which we live. The blend is not always easy, and Nicoletto does not delude us into thinking the matter a quick study, that new cosmology is simply standard cosmology refurbished. In the reflections offered here, Nicoletto chooses his language with great care, each word helping us to understand more clearly and deeply the insights he would share. Though each homily stands on its own, readers will hear, over the span of them, certain themes repeated and reexpressed, able to open the

Scripture reading in ways that will surprise and please. Cosmogenesis challenges Christians' long-established sense of a personal God. And yet, as we read on, we can feel consoled that the classic and intense imagery of so many biblical passages is deeply suitable to our Universe—multiverse—identity and roots. Pushing us beyond our traditional sense of stewardship and human governance of the world to a deeper and more respectful sense of our place within creation, we learn how deeply suited is the biblical tradition to much of what we hear emerging in the cosmological conversation. Christian believers will find themselves challenged by both the liturgical readings and the fresh cosmology to a more intense ethical praxis. We can think of no better way for third-millennium Christians to be drawn into the stories that shape our lives in ways we have, perhaps, scarcely begun to understand than to explore the great mystery in which all creation-partners live.

Barbara Green, OP
Professor of Biblical Studies
Dominican School of Philosophy
    and Theology
Graduate Theological Union
Berkeley, California

Sandra M. Schneiders, IHM
Professor (emerita) of New
    Testament Studies and
    Spirituality
Jesuit School of Theology of
    Santa Clara University
Berkeley, California

Acknowledgments

How do we interpret the Scripture in light of the new Universe story? How do we participate with our lives in the creative and sacred Action who continues to be at work in the evolutionary process of the world? These two questions are at the origin of this book, *Journey of Faith, Journey of the Universe*, which aims to interweave the discovery of the immensity of our expanding Universe, the Word that every Sunday is proclaimed in our congregations, and the involvement of the entire Earth community in this ongoing and unfinished creation.

I am very grateful for the help, appreciation, and encouragement that I have received from many people. In particular I thank Sr. Barbara Green, OP, who first spurred me to embark on this project that she has supported all along the way, and to Liturgical Press, which consented to the adventure. I express my deepest appreciation to Kristin Burke, who has consistently edited with care during these last three years the texts that now appear in unity. I am thankful to Carrie Rehak for her inexhaustible enthusiasm and passion that make things happen. Last but not least, my deepest acknowledgment to my monastic community of Incarnation Monastery, especially Fr. Andrew Colnaghi, that allowed me to prepare, voice, and offer these meditations.

As we learn from the story of the Universe, nothing grows in isolation and selfishness, but everything unfolds in connection, relationship, and interdependence. In the same way I am indebted to many travel companions that have enlightened, widened, and inspired my perspective. I desire to mention especially Brian T. Swimme and Mary

Evelyn Tucker—whose book, *Journey of the Universe*, has inspired the title and the fervor of the present volume—as well as Judy Cannato, Elizabeth A. Johnson, Ilia Delio, Richard Rohr, and Caroline Baker. The reader who wants to engage with their works will find a list at the end of the book called "Inspirational Sources."

Finally, I hope that the reader may discover oneself to be part of the great flow that began with the big bang of matter, and enfolded in life, consciousness, and love. Above all, I wish that we may consent to welcome the ineffable Mystery peeping out in our own lives, calling us to participate in a cosmic and eucharistic banquet that draws together all existing beings.

Second Sunday of Advent
Isa 11:1-10; Rom 15:4-9; Matt 3:1-12

Advent comes today with an engrossing and unsettling call for us: *Prepare the way.* Isn't it a surprise to discover ourselves solicited not just to walk along a path already trod, tested, and known, but *to become a way* for something or someone unknown and uncontainable, who is about to come into the world, thanks to the welcoming space we prepare? We are not irrelevant or uniform matter of the world. Each one of us, no matter where and how we are, is involved in the possibility of this coming, asked to become channels of such manifestations of justice, compassion, and peace. And we are not alone in this risky preparation that presses in upon the present. We have been preceded by a *myriad* of beings. We are called in the wake of Noah and Abraham, Jesse, David, and Isaiah, Ruth, Mary the mother of Jesus, Mary the beloved, and the passionate believers of all ages, races, religions, and cultures.

We could say that the *entire* creation, from the initial, great flaring forth, is *preparing the way*, is involved in a birthing process. Perhaps the world is this perennial, incomplete, unfulfilled birth that is about to happen at every moment, thanks to earthly and celestial beings: light and water, sun and moon, stars and trees, birds, cow, calf, lion, and asp, together with our technologies and arts. We are part of an enormous, continuous birth from matter, to life, to consciousness, to self-consciousness, and to love. All creatures are preparing the way, participating in the birth of Christ who was, is, and is to come. We are also involved in birthing Christ, now that Jesus has performed his song of love, has released his Spirit upon us, and has sent us to incarnate the advent of love in any appropriate and inappropriate circumstances.

Christ is on his way of fulfillment through everybody, widening through us, in an all-embracing and creative compassion. However, we experience this not as an easy birth. The preparation wails through the birth pangs, contradictions, and conflicts of the world. We know there are wounds, demises, hostilities, deadlocks, darkness, resistances, failures, and cries at every stage of the journey of the Universe, of our personal and communal history. There are despairs such as those mentioned by the prophet Isaiah, when a small group of people goes back from Babylon to a destroyed Jerusalem: Who will have the courage to go back, to start, to sow, to hope again? Likewise, there is an anesthetized and lifeless religion in the holy city of Jerusalem at the time of John the Baptist. The religious leaders are lulling themselves in the comfort zone of rules, privileges, and power: Who will embody the passionate and transformative power of the hidden Source of all creativity and compassion?

We also live in threatening times at this turning point in our global civilization. Forces of consumptions, injustice, oppression, and exclusion are working against efforts to build a life-sustaining society and are destroying planet Earth. Who will embody the radical transformations we so urgently need? What is amazing is that an insistent, persistent voice continues to resound, ferment, encourage, and unsettle in the deserts of humanity and of earth: *Prepare the way.*

Unexpected ways are germinating, as they are eagerly desired, invoked, and enacted. A transformation, a new beginning, sprouts from the hidden below: from the margins, from the pain, and by the power of imagination, dialogue, faith, and hope. Abraham goes out of his land toward a promised fecundity. Rosa Parks decides not to give up her bus seat to a white person, initiating a new era in civil rights. The Buddha leaves his rich palace, setting out on a journey of liberation. John the Baptist renounces the status quo in favor of a journey to the sources of wilderness. Jesus disarms by great love the powers of death. Nelson Mandela as a servant of justice dismantles the system of apartheid.

How are we preparing the coming of compassion, justice, and peace in the daily gestures, choices, and relationships of our lives?

We have been baptized with the Holy Spirit and with fire. *Fire* is the passionate love song, sung at the heart of our Earth, of our consciousness. Paul the apostle voices the effects of this fire: togetherness, welcoming one another, our mutual belonging in the living body of the Earth and of the Universe.

Let us tune to the love song of the coming Christ at the heart of
        our time,
    let us reclaim the world in all its richness and intensity.
Let us *hope* in ever new beginnings, as Gregory of Nyssa[1] boldly
        claims:
    Hope always draws the soul
    from the beauty which is seen to what is beyond,
    always kindles the desire for the hidden
    through what is constantly perceived,
    without cessation or satiety of the desire.

Note

1. Gregory of Nyssa, *Life of Moses*, trans. Abraham J. Malherbe and Everett Ferguson, Classics of Western Spirituality series (New York: Paulist, 1978), 114.

Christmas
(Mass during the Day)

Isa 52:7-10; Heb 1:1-6; John 1:1-18

Today a great light has come upon the earth.

What a boldness, a nerve, an unbridled imagination is witnessed by John's prologue, joining the creative energy of God's word, through whom the Universe continues to unfurl, to the human and messy embodiment of Jesus Christ, manifestation of God's glory, imprint of God's being. What has this divine, dazzling light to do with our daily, troubled, and sometimes unbearable life? Today, when we still are in the wreckage of financial, ecological, and communicative crises, this light shines on the contradictions of our personal and communal joy and pain, hope and despair.

We pause for a moment on the light, on the tent, and on the heart.

The light. The Universe unfolded from a hot point, a common cosmic source, an initial free and creative event, particles of matter and light expanding in an endless adventure. We have been suffused with and accompanied by light since the beginning of time through a very long, winding, and risky journey. The light becoming Sun has been the wellspring of the atmosphere of our planet, and of all living beings. And then the light of consciousness emerged, the light radiating in our languages, cultures, gestures, rituals, arts, and technologies. At a certain moment of this cosmic and unfinished story, this infinite light has built its receptive body, converges and shines in that point of conjunction of light and love, of human and divine that is a historical being: Jesus, a vulnerable, contestable, and disposable body. At once it is given to us to contemplate the mighty force that is birthing the Cosmos and shines in the defenseless and tender flesh of a baby. A body that will be ruthlessly torn apart on the cross and will release the Spirit beyond boundaries and limitations in all directions. The divine light creatively embraces tensions, paradoxes, and contradictions, the glories and humiliations of the flesh.

The tent. The all-nourishing and still-in-the-making Word pitches his tent among us. From the beginning, a nomadic, experimental God provokes an uncontainable swirling of particles, galaxies, and planets, spirals of DNA, bursts of thoughts and emotions, swarms of cultures, and hurricanes of technological, digital networks. The Word, emerging as Atman, *Ruah*, Law, Enlightenment, and Sophia, is always tabernacling with God's creation, with God's people, with the ever-changing human perceptions of God's inexhaustible names and shapes.[1] She is opening our senses to ever-new dimensions of consciousness and breaking the walls that are blocking the uncontainable expansion of the infinite Light. We contemplate Jesus as a precarious tent, as a host and a guest without possession, as an exposed and begging word, without religious and institutional security, and identified with those who camp on the edges, follow the star, believe in transformation, yearn for justice and hope, and are patiently open to love's promise.

The heart. This holy day has the potential to reconnect us with what matters most: the holiness of our heart, the heart of holiness beating at the heart of each one of us, and of all creatures, and of the Cosmos. This heart's light shines and asks to be received, to become embracing love, but we can decide differently: we can raise walls of separation around Jerusalem, around our hearts, countries, and communities, becoming impervious to her brilliance and transforming compassion. What path will we choose to follow? A path according to the encompassing, enlightening Word, a path of justice and peace, or the one of extinction and violence?

Today a great light has come upon the earth
yet not so striking, not so blinding to force us
but hidden in the folds of a baby,
mixed in daily gestures of healing, attention, and compassion.
Exposed to the winds of our freedom,

she is easily killed by violence and deceit,
yet always rising
in faith, hope, and love.

Note

1. John Shelby Spong, *The Fourth Gospel: Tales of a Jewish Mystic* (New York: Harper One, 2014), 46–47.

Baptism of the Lord

Isa 42:1-4, 6-7; Acts 10:34-38; Matt 3:13-17

The heavens were opened to him
and he saw the Spirit of God alighting on him.

Let us open the heavens of our imagination. Imagine the feeling of immensity sensed by the astronomer Edwin Hubble when, using the Hooker telescope on Mount Wilson, he discovered a multitude of creative galaxies existing beyond our Milky Way galaxy, thought to be the only existing one. Even more astonishing, he discovered that our Universe is endlessly expanding in all directions, turning our image of a settled Cosmos upside down. The heavens are not fixed but ceaselessly opening, widening, and transforming. The heavens embed us into a creative, mysterious, and evolutionary Cosmos.

Imagine how the change of a political or spiritual guide often open the heavens for a large community in the world, igniting and liberating frozen possibilities, potentialities, hopes, and pressing needs. Imagine ourselves as children, when heavens after heavens of wonder and discovery were opened for us as we experienced the fragrance and the threat of our emerging realities: worlds of senses, tastes, feelings, words, and people. Imagine the heavens that open when the fire of prayer ignites in our hearts, and the eyes of contemplation are opened, and we perceive our life in a new perspective, from the side of God's compassionate love.

We participate in the opening of heavens in many ways. The texture, the grain, the melody of reality is never closed and uniform; it rather resembles an overflowing of living waters in which we are immersed, and from which we emerge. There are many heavens, layers of life, quantum leaps, levels of matter and spirit, openings of consciousness that expand and unite us in a chorus of differences.

What is this invisible, elusive element that opens the heavens of the journey of the Universe, of our planet Earth, of our personal and communal experience? We are opened from within by an invisible, merciful Spirit that ascends in us and alights on us: a hidden and unbounded heart, yet manifested and embodied as processes of birthing, liberation, and healing that are revealed in the narratives of cultures, religions, and the story of the Universe.

The heavens were opened
and a voice from the heavens said, this is my cherished epiphany of love.

Within Christmastide we participated in a symphony of openings, of relationships between earth and heaven, human and divine: visions and visitations of angels, revelatory dreams, wombs of possibilities, guiding stars, a promising child. Today, in a meaningful gesture, Jesus plunges into the height and the abyss of our humanity and of creation. He passes through the constraining walls of our bodies, souls, and cultures, walls raised by fears and cemented by violence, injustice, and exclusions. He crosses the hardened places of our hearts, our brokenness, agony, and despairs. He traverses the extreme experience of abandonment: My God, why have you abandoned me?

He passes through a crucifixion, the magnified network of evil, and paradox thickens. As Richard Rohr notices, the more light, the more mystery and darkness; the more love, the more hatred. And yet the heavens of love were opened to him, a voice comes from the hidden heart. *A voice: my beloved* (Song 2:8). The same pleased voice that at the beginning of creation repeatedly exclaims, *It is good, it is very good* (Gen 1:1-31). Jesus incarnates the crumbling of walls that block the infinite light hidden within creation; he is transformed into the mystery of arising Love that nourishes meaning, hope, and faith, attracting us out of the tomb toward an unfurling fullness of love that supports everything—even death.

Birthed from above, moving through death into life, each one of us incarnates the Universe surging into existence anew, generated by the invisible element of love that we seek, the hidden heart that finds us because it loves us. In our time we plunge into a new, dramatic baptism of human evolution. An openness is needed to see: a new level of consciousness and care is required for this moment in which we are destroying our Earth.

Is it possible that the immense journey of the Universe and of the spirit blossoming in our human consciousness will lead to destruction? To destruction or to a loving purpose, according to the hidden heart of Life? We need, we invoke, we offer our bodies for the birth on Earth of the divine element, of a vision of wholeness, of an action of inclusion of all our planet Earth.

The heavens were opened
and a voice said, this is my cherished epiphany of love.

Fifth Sunday in Ordinary Time

Isa 58:7-10; 1 Cor 2:1-5; Matt 5:13-16

The prophet Isaiah, the apostle Paul, and the Son of humanity, Jesus, speak of a light that *shall* break forth from the darkness of oppression, of the wisdom of the cross, and of a salt that can lose its taste. They each express awareness of constraints, bleakness, and tastelessness in the historical moment of their lives. We may also experience depletion of meaning in our personal life or, on a larger scale, in the exhaustion of planetary resources, in the disintegration of social bonds, and in the predominance of individual or corporative interests. In modern times even the name of God has lost its taste for many people, mainly because of our use or abuse of it as a defense and cover of interests, structures, or old wineskins. And yet the good news that resounds today is that we can become the salt, the yeast, and the taste-givers of the Earth. How can it happen?

Let us listen to a poetic meditation by Mary Oliver, "First Happenings":[1]

> A morning-glory morning with its usual glory,
> dawn particularly startling with citrons and
> mauves, petunias in the garden flashing their
> tender signals of gratitude. The sunflowers
> creak in their glass-colored dresses. Cosmos,
> the four o'clocks, the sweet alyssum nod to
> the roses who so very politely nod back.
>
> And now it is time to go to work. At my desk
> I look out over the fluttering petals, little
> fires. Each one fresh and almost but not quite
> replicable.

Consider wearing such a satisfying body!
Consider being, with your entire self, such
a quiet prayer!

Just an ordinary sliver of time, an attentive look at the garden, a listening heart, and—suddenly—an explosion of tasty joy radiates in naming and feeling the multicolored flowers, as if each one of them has a soul, is an epiphany, an embodied prayer. With careful attention, the poet makes herself a hospitable vessel where the creatures reveal their inner vibrations, their surplus of splendor: their flavor. We pay new attention to the hidden work of flowers themselves. We have in fact discovered how they found an amazing way to season the world, how they became catalyst of beauty and life in our planet. With creative intelligence and many attempts, they were able to transform light into an extraordinary symphony of life through the process of photosynthesis.

The Sun has always enlightened our planet, but there was no recipient, no organ able to receive the solar energy and convert it into the food we eat, the oxygen we breathe, and the beauty of trees and flowers that surround us. The Earth and the Universe found through photosynthesis a way to express themselves more magnificently, and to flavor the body of the world. The same was done by the first multicellular beings, awakening the wonder of life on Earth. At a certain point in the evolutionary journey something happened: an uncontrollable energy overflowed in a particular species, a new fever in the human that boiled over into the world as symbolic consciousness,[2] words, mental forms, imagination, creative gestures, dance, and rituals. Humans began to flavor Earth with arts and crafts, knowledge and wisdom, cooperation and cults, science and technologies.

Between all these flavors that creatively made the world tasty, the Universe was able to express Jesus as a manifestation of God's gratuitous and rising compassion. Jesus is a tremendous storyteller; his parables season the soil of our lives and awaken us to the radical sense of grace that touches and flavors each being. Each of us remembers the parables of the birds in the sky and the lilies of the field, reminding us that we can know everything, have everything, control everything; but if there is no deep trust in the inner wellspring of love, we create a cold desert, deprived of meaning, beauty, and creative passion. Similar to the process of photosynthesis, Jesus is able to transform even death, illness, and violence into a poem of life and of love.

In every Eucharist we renew the seasoning of the world: bread and wine, fruits of the Earth and of human participation become the body and blood of God shared with all, All-nourishing source of compassion for all and each one of us. What are the sources of taste, of meaning, of passion in each one of us? Are we able to pay attention and to name—as does Mary Oliver—all the living creatures that at every moment surround and season us? Are we willing—as Jesus did—to share with others the gifts we embody in this unique adventure of our life?

That we may wear like the lilies of the field such a satisfying body!

That we may become, with our entire selves, a quiet prayer!

Notes

1. Mary Oliver, "First Happenings," in *New and Selected Poems*, vol. 2 (Boston: Beacon, 2005), 8.

2. Brian Thomas Swimme and Mary Evelyn Tucker, *Journey of the Universe* (New Haven, CT: Yale University Press, 2011).

First Sunday of Lent

Gen 2:7-9; 3:1-7; Rom 5:12-19; Matt 4:1-11

We are grateful that we have not only natural seasons that give rhythm to the year but also symbolic, ritual, liturgical seasons that nourish and enlighten our pilgrimage of faith on Earth, connecting us with the creative God of the past, of the present, and of the future. With Ash Wednesday as an initiatory gateway we have entered into the forty-day season of Lent, stretching toward the paschal mystery of passion, death, and resurrection of Christ, and to the exceeding gift of his Spirit at Pentecost.

As we know from history, the liturgical season of Lent was formed as a journey of those repenting for having fallen away from love, and a journey of catechumens—those who desire to be initiated to the Christian life through the immersion into the deep waters of love of the Easter Vigil, the rebirth into the resurrected Christ. The liturgical atmosphere that accompanies us in our Lenten exodus is marked by invitations and practices for our daily lives that aim toward conversion, empathic listening, transformation, reconciliation, restored relationships, and the abundant gift of life that God intends for all.

Today's narratives from the First and Second Testaments present dramatic scenarios of how our ways of life impact all forms of life and of creation. The primordial scene in the garden of Genesis and the temptations of Jesus in the desert tell us about the corrosive power of suspicion that creeps into our minds or hearts, which the Bible literally calls *demonic*, splitting or divisive because it insinuates the doubt that we are not really safe in God, that God is unreliable. What kind of image is the demonic power acting in our ethical, political, economic, and spiritual assumptions that we project onto God? Satan suggests to our personal and collective experience that the all-nourishing and supporting Mystery is hiding something from us. The Ground of all beings is protecting a source of power that he doesn't want to share with us and that we need to conquer in order to live, to be autonomous, immortal.

We are persuaded to be *afraid* of God as a threatening, competitive, and despotic presence. The radical temptation seems to consist in a rejection, in a denial of our mortality, contingency, and vulnerability, making sure that we are the controlling and measuring source of our existence and of the world. The devil in the garden or in the desert of our time continues to unfold inexhaustible arsenals of appealing needs and desires, all of them suggesting that we miss something that we have to conquer for the sake of our safety, be it the fruits of the tree, food, defense, dominion, or prestige.

Although we do not intend harm, this spiral of self-assurance may become an *uncreating* rhythm: through myriad forms of human power and ecological degradation we are disrupting a fundamental quality of God's garden—its life-generating capacity, producing increasing economic violence on many people and on the planet Earth. Even most sacred dimensions of human experience can be exploited by this demonic logic. Religions and religious laws have repeatedly used the name of God as a weapon to smash the lives of people, to exclude them from the community, or to control behavior through fear and authority.

The good news or, as Paul says, *the abundance of God's grace* is that in Jesus God manifests God's totally gratuitous self-bestowing love, God's love for the finite, unfinished, groaning, suffering world. In Jesus the *radical temptation* to reject our vulnerability and be immortal and almighty like God is turned upside down by the *radical incarnation* of the divine love. Jesus, God's manifestation, becomes the flesh we reject. The flesh assumed in Jesus enters in solidarity with the very texture of our biological existence, with all material Universe, and with all the damaged, violated, wounded bodies of creation. The contingent, unfinished, and groaning world becomes a part of God's *own* divine story, including the suffering death of the beloved Son of humanity. Christ tastes in his death what it means to suffer and agonize for love of the world. In his passion, God knows the pain and death of the mortal flesh, and through faith God opens us to the creative power of God's divine love in the resurrection of Jesus' disfigured body.[1]

Today, for the first time in human history, the future of life in our planet lies in our hands. This First Sunday of Lent reminds us not to trust in the seduction of fear, power, control, hostility, and consumption, but rather embrace the ineffable God who gives life, freedom, friendship, hope, and communion among all creatures.

How do we feel about our relationship with the Ultimate Reality of God: Is it inspired by trust and surrender or by threat and fear? How do we relate with other people, creatures, earthly reality—as partner or prey, as friend or enemy?

All-generative and gratuitous Womb
we enjoy the freedom we have been given,
and the compassion that shined in Jesus.
We desire to become love in human form,
to take on responsibility and care
for the planet Earth
and for all her blossoming beings.

Note

1. I invite the reader to expand the meaning of *deep incarnation* by plunging into the pages that have inspired this meditation: Elizabeth A. Johnson, *Ask the Beasts: Darwin and the God of Love* (London: Continuum, 2014), 192–206.

Year A

Third Sunday of Lent

Exod 17:3-7; Rom 5:1-2, 5-8; John 4:5-42

After the experience of temptation and of transfiguration, this Third Sunday of Lent draws us into an adventurous journey of faith, toward the living water of the Spirit, source of perennial life. As Paul magnificently synthesizes it, *the love of God has been poured out into our hearts through the Holy Spirit of Christ.*

Both the scene of the Israelites in their exodus through the desert and of the meeting of Jesus with the Samaritan woman at the well of Sychar express a basic need of life: the necessity of water. Water is the condition for life: our bodies, like many earthly creatures, cannot live without it. Water inhabits our flesh, circulates through our veins, and drenches our tissues as it also flows through and vivifies our planet Earth.

Our bodies not only need water but are woven by a great variety of thirsts, desires, and passions that shape us into the sort of people we become. We are thirsty for water and meaning, love and knowledge, good relationships and freedom, healthy environment and justice, beauty and happiness. Thirst is a powerful force that moves, orients, and pushes us forward, toward a source that can fulfill it. Thirsts and desires keep open the doors of our body for something other that we seek or yearn: they point to a gap that wants to be filled. Only a thirsting, incomplete, open being is capable of love.

Our journey of faith may begin with a need, a thirst, or a request to be quenched. Over the journey, like the Samaritan woman, we are often called to uncover the deepest thirsts of our hearts, to access another quality of water: living, breathing water. Jesus asks the woman for some water. But now, surprisingly, he manifests an emergent quality of water: *a living water* that he *will give, and will become in her*

16

a spring of water gushing up to eternal life. It is a birth through the waters of the unconditional, divine Love, because *God is love* (1 John 4:8) and Christ is the open depth within each one of us. *A spring of water gushing up to eternal life* suggests that in every person there is a speck, a point of soul, a vital spark connected with the divine and with our flowing experience. At the heart of our being we carry a God-shaped hole. But we can block the flowing of these waters, as Etty Hillesum says: "One must clear the path toward You in him/herself, God, and if only you make certain that your path to God is unblocked, then you can keep renewing yourself at these inner sources."[1]

Jesus mentions the stones, the limits, or the barriers that separate the life of the Samaritan woman from the living water. There is, in fact, a series of "husbands," of relationships the woman had, that didn't work: perhaps an allusion to the many marriages of the Samaritan people with diverse religious cults. What are our personal and communal barriers and divides that need to be acknowledged? They can be the unmasking of destructive, unhealthy forces or habits within us. They can be our irresponsible and foolish drives that are destroying our planet Earth. They can be the unredeemed and excluding attitudes of our churches, religions, politics, and economies.

The good news is that even our wants, deficiencies, limits, griefs, or shadows can become *passages* of the Whole that exceeds our expectations, needs, and possibilities.

Divine Love deepens and expands time, world, soul; she works from within, opens us to a beyond out of our control, out of our grasp, and out of our planning. It is the gratuitous work of *Grace*.

As soon as the Samaritan woman perceives there is something spiritual, fresh, and creative about Jesus, she asks him the hot-button divisive religious issue of her time: "Which mountain do you worship on, this mountain or that mountain, Gerizim or Jerusalem?" The woman poses the limited alternative between stone temples and places, but Jesus does something absolutely fascinating: as a barrier-breaker, he draws us beyond human barriers, divides, and prejudices and says, *"Woman, a time is coming, and now is, when it won't matter which mountain you worship on. Because what God is looking for are people who will worship in spirit and in truth."*

Worship *in spirit and truth* is an experience of union and openness in love with the divine Mystery within our souls and within the heart of the Universe. "Divine love," says the Franciscan theologian Ilia Delio, "is not a river of stagnant water but a fountain full of overflowing love, love that is forever awakening to new life. God is ever newness in love and the power of everything new in love."[2] Jesus, in his extreme gesture of self-giving love, the cross, will become a source of blood and water, embodying the deep waters of God's mystery whose Love loves us first. The more deeply we enter into this living water, the more deeply we enter into the heart of the divine Source, who radiates through all the Universe, who supports the vast and expanding web of life.

Today we are at a tipping point, finding ourselves in the midst of vast destruction that is at the same time a moment of profound creativity. We have confidence that between tension and opposing forces the creative Spirit that moves and breathes within us and in the Universe will inspire us and guide us into the living waters of the future. How can we participate in the flow of living waters in our daily life, in our relationships, choices, and actions? Can we promote openness to the world, express our feeling of kinship with the vast symphony of the Universe, with peoples, trees and animals, waters and air?

At noon, on the cross, the Son of Humanity will also ask for water:
I am thirsty (John 19:28).
You are continually thirsty for our love, God:
that we may become the waters
of your compassionate and relational heart.
That we may receive the Spirit of a new human consciousness
that binds all beings and manifestations of existence.
That we may be your radiance
at the heart of the Universe.

Notes

1. Etty Hillesum, *An Interrupted Life* (New York: Henry Holt, 1996), 218.
2. Ilia Delio, *The Unbearable Wholeness of Being: God, Evolution, and the Power of Love* (Maryknoll, NY: Orbis, 2013), 76.

Fourth Sunday of Lent

1 Sam 16:1b, 6-7, 10-13a; Eph 5:8-14; John 9:1-41

In his revolutionary book *On the Origin of Species*, Charles Darwin describes his first descent from the *Beagle* onto the distant Cape Verde islands. He concludes his day of fascinating observations on local birds and flowers with an astounded response: "It has been for me a glorious day, like giving a blind man eyes." The readings of this Fourth Sunday of Lent orbit around the opening of eyes to a born-blind man, the giving of heart-sight that pierces the outward appearances, and the passage from darkness to light.

Jesus' gift of sight to a blind man and the attentive and caring gaze of Darwin—a gaze captivated by how all species of organisms looked, functioned, and interrelated with each other—open us to the wonder of seeing, to the emergence of the eye and all its rich potentialities in the tapestry of life. Until a certain moment there was in fact no sight in the Universe. Yet, it seems that the invention of the eye was not an accident: There was a need, a desire pulsing at the heart of life to see, to reflect on itself, and to deepen its awareness.[1] The whole tree of life was going to find a way to see. We can trace the attempts of this desire in the several times that life tried to invent eyesight, beginning with an eye created by trilobites made out of mineral calcite to an entirely new type of water-based eye invented by worms and fish, which is the eye we inherited.

But the human capacity of our eyes is not a finished form; they continue to unfold and evolve, exploring the outer and inner spaces, because we also want to know, to understand deeply, to improve our power of observation, to sharpen the quality, extension, and intensity of seeing. Sight became insight: the capacity to see in the inner screen of imagination and to relate to the surrounding world with attentive and empathic care. A new way of seeing came into being in the human, a symbolic consciousness that ignites our imagination and creativity, allowing us to externalize our eyes in languages and forms, numbers, techniques, dreams, and cultures, and to be amazed by the exuberance of life.[2] This empowered sight gives us the capacity to extend our vision into the depths of time, from the initial and gratuitous big bang to the edges of the Cosmos; to explore the subatomic world of particles; to envision our social, ethical, and religious choices in a planetary perspective.

With the expansion of our biological eyes through art, science, technology, and digital devices our human mind has changed radically over the course of history: We have seized control of life, taken matter into our own hands. We have become able to radically alter the Earth's atmosphere and general climatic conditions: We have become a *geophysical force*. And we are now beginning to manipulate life itself, including the genetic makeup of human beings. Because we humans are playing a cosmic role, we experience how important and urgent it is in a changing world to be healed in our eyes. Our conceptions and behaviors that were perhaps appropriate in previous contexts of life now hold the danger of creating a destructive blindness, an inability to reinvent and to direct the present form of the world. We need eyes, visions, and worldviews that renew the meaning and purpose of our personal, collective, and universal lives in a time when our planet is threatened by ecological collapse, marked disparity, and sectarian violence.

The Swiss sculptor Alberto Giacometti wrote that although we all have eyes, those that the oculist tests and controls, few are the eyes, that is to say *our* eyes, that are able to be messengers of something particularly meaningful, namely, that of a glance. Often, the meeting with a person happens first through a look, before any word. By the way a person feels oneself seen and by the way we look at another person, forms of authentic contact can be opened or, on the contrary, cold and insensitive walls are built, destined to extinguish every meeting.

Today's readings point to the emergence of spiritual, embodied, inclusive eyes, the eyes of divine consciousness that widens our heart-sight and transforms our darkness into light. In the healing of a man born blind we are exposed to the compassionate gaze of God as it is mirrored in the look of Jesus, who is the eyes, the self-giving light of God. In Jesus a new consciousness of God emerged, a new inclusive sight able to embrace vulnerability and death, to become sensitive to the groaning of creatures for more freedom and love. In a sort of new creation from the primordial mud—he smears the clay on the eyes of the blind—Jesus opens in us the eyes of God, eyes that are a work in process, whereas the agency of divine Wisdom never relents, and never stops urging, expanding, and appealing to the wellspring of Light.

We are journeying toward the paschal mystery, the crucified love as the manifestation of God's radical passion. Perhaps to *follow* Jesus, to enter into his light, means for us to be ignited by his creative and divine passion. We surrender to this element of immensity that acts in our hearts, opening us to the vision of a sacred and living Universe; of a participative and cocreative action with the whole planet Earth; of a dialoguing spirituality among wisdoms, religions, knowledge(s), genders, races, and expertise.

What is the quality of our seeing the world from a planetary dimension: Is it an attentive sensitivity and a loving care? What does the eye of the Spirit want us to see in this moment of evolution, and for the next evolution of life on planet Earth?

Flow of light,
of freedom, of love
open in us eyes
doors to the deeper worlds
of compassion, wonder, and creativeness
to continue the journey
of the Universe, of the Earth
in their astounding, staggering exuberance,
in their fullness yet to come.

Notes

1. Brian Thomas Swimme and Mary Evelyn Tucker, *Journey of the Universe* (New Haven, CT: Yale University Press, 2011).
2. Ibid., 61–66.

Year A

Easter Vigil
Rom 6:3-11; Matt 28:1-10

We enter into the cave of this night,
and we are transformed by Grace into the flame of her light.

It seems like a long, endless night since we entered the last supper, woven by betrayal, violence, injustice, and abandonment, sealed in the end with the stone of death—then silence, mourning, and blackness. We have the feeling it is a not-so-distant, alien night: it continues to enshroud us. We are extending this night with our numberless and mortal actions. It is like we are digging a planetary tomb that encompasses oceans and skies, soaking it with pollution, inequality, destructiveness, and brutality.

In this all-embracing night of the planet and of the soul we have been drawn by grief and hope around the tomb, the buried body of Jesus, where the sky of God's love shone when he was alive, and that the violence of the world hastened to choke to death.

We began piling up wood on the brazier, wood of tenderness, despair, misery, and the groaning of creation, of all living beings. In the tomb of this night Someone lights a fire, as was done on the first day of creation. Someone budges the overwhelming stone, impossible for us to move. Something unprecedented emerges in the Cosmos, an unknown Universe is open inside this world. Someone has entered creation, our heart, a life-changing Energy has penetrated our inmost flesh, has transfigured our biological existence, provoked a leap of consciousness. The external, punitive, separate God has collapsed, and the human becomes the vessel in which the divine continues to blossom, to expand, and to take care of the world. The daybreak can no more be retained by guards, controllers, temples, creeds, and norms.

An earthquake—the world is turned upside down.

We enter into the cave of this night,
and we are transformed by Grace into the flame of her light.

In each one of us transpires now the very fragrance of boundless freedom and love, living waters that overflow the limited maps of our knowledge. Jesus finally free-falls into the larger, boundless Source of compassion, and we with him have entered into the very heart of God, into what has yet to be imagined. Collapsing into blackness, and *there* finding light was the experience of the apostle Paul, when he was caught in the crucible of Grace. No surprise that women and men for several days are traumatized: struck dumb with fear, disbelief, and astonishment. New life is not a joke; it is, first, dissolution.

We can be frightened because our protective frontiers, comfort zone, cherished and safety customs have melted in love. All that has held us in place is gone, swept away. In the dying of separations we surrender. We find ourselves living into the life of God, in communion with all creatures. We feel that the Spirit is now working in us, that we have much more power, consciousness, and responsibility with regard to all sentient beings and creation. We are invited by this Night to walk the path of the cosmic Christ because divine Compassion has opened the eyes of our heart, showing us that we are of the same, eternal stuff of God. We have entered into God's unfathomable mystery, and we have become vessels and agents of the life-giving Spirit. Is our faith rooted deep enough in God's love to sustain us through demise and darkness? As raised bodies do we honor the divine Breath in each creature and in all creation?

This night reveals to the world
Your subversive economics of gift:
all loss, and no return.
This night links you, Jesus, with all life,
with transformation and intimacy beyond imagining.
This night reveals the fragility of our faith:
never accomplished,
exposed to God's passionate excess.
May we be present, love generously,

and our tears of sorrow, grief, and separation
be transformed in tears of joy.
May we enter into the cave of this night,
and be transformed by Grace into the flame of your light.

Fifth Sunday of Easter

Acts 6:1-7; 1 Pet 2:4-9; John 14:1-12

In this Fifth Sunday of Easter Jesus adds another color to the *I AMs* prism that is accompanying us into the fulfillment of Pentecost: *I am the way, the truth, and the life.* Like oxygen for living beings, the community of the Fourth Gospel compares their transformational experience of Jesus to the way, the truth, and the life. With his self-giving love until death, Jesus showed them the face of the unseen, divine Mystery so that in his humanity they could sense, taste, enjoy, and share in the eternity of God. We also believe and experience that God continues to be met in the living Christ as way, truth, and life because he is at the heart of our personal and cosmic life: where Jesus is, there we are also.

Can we interpret this revelation of Jesus as way, truth, and life in a more expansive time frame, from a cosmic, evolutionary perspective? If we look at the immense journey of the Universe, we are overcome with astonishment by the innumerable *ways* the Cosmos invented to expand, connect, and shape *life*. How could it happen, this incessant and ongoing creative process from the initial formation of molecules to the enormous spirals of galaxies, from the lowliest bacteria to the highest hominid, to the amazing overabundance of flying, swimming, smelling, singing, barking, mating, nursing, fighting, praying, and dying that surrounds us?

What we have discovered is that the Universe and Earth are *alive*, they bring to life, and they evolve. Earth organizes herself, spins, interweaves, acts, and generates all the lives and the rhythms of the living beings. Her wholeness and grandeur is present in each particular event, in each individual creature, in our own personal and collective self. Just consider how the Earth built a way for sentient

25

and sensuous life (thanks to the prokaryotes' activity), creating an atmosphere with the right concentration of oxygen—neither more nor less—so as to provide the potential nest to host all the animal species.

Then the ebullient, restless Universe opened another, more complex way of life—through humans—to reflect on itself, to arise the quest for meaning, beauty, truth, purpose, and wonder. Think of the tremendous labor of all living forms that have adventurously traveled to arrive finally at us. And today, with our techno-sciences and bio-technologies, the Cosmos is perhaps opening the way of *conscious evolution*. We are on the brink of reshaping our inherited bodily and human form, to leap beyond our genetic limits, to create something unknown that has never existed before. With our system of production, the advanced global capitalism, we are even planning to destroy the Earth. We listen, daily, to alarming reports on our terrifying influence on our planet. In 2014, two teams of scientists released papers concerning the West Antarctic Ice Sheet melt. The study showed that glacial melt is faster than predicted, and in an unstoppable way that means global sea levels are to rise more than was figured.

We are living today an ambivalent and dramatic truth, a combination of hope and despair: We are following the instinct to transcend, the impulse that moves the sublime achievements of human heart, mind, and imagination to a new cosmic frontier, and at the same time we are wasting all our sources of life. Does Jesus' saying *I am the way, the truth, and the life* generate alternative worldviews and practices? Does he contribute something as essential to the Earth's life as oxygen?

As we mentioned at the beginning, Jesus is called the way, the truth, and the life in response to the quest of the community that generated the Fourth Gospel. They came to experience in his passionate and longing humanity the overcoming of many limits that their religious and cultural environment had built, boundaries that Jesus experienced as an obstacle from the living, exploring, all-embracing God he was moved by. Cultural, religious, and moral containers are all transcended in favor of a deeper, wider, and richer access to life, and life in abundance, as expressed in the revelatory *signs* of the Fourth Gospel, and in *the* sign of the crucified/glorified God. Extraordinarily enough, even Jesus' suffering and death are not interpreted as an end but rather believed as a new beginning, a new consciousness of the living God that is no more an external presence but is discovered as a raising force at the heart of the human and of creation.[1]

The life-enhancing power of love that the disciples met in Jesus is now acting, breathing in their lives, is their pulsing truth, has become the ever-expanding, creative, healing power of their lives. No surprise is Peter's enthusiasm, expressed in our second reading: in Christ you are "a chosen race, a royal priesthood," living stones in the sight of God so that, as Richard Rohr says, "The soul is God's 'I AM' continued in [you]," the part of you that "already knows, desires, and truly seeks God."[2]

Christ consciousness, his Spirit at work in our hearts and in the Universe, is always looking for embodied ways on Earth, and the Acts of the Apostles give us today a taste of this enacting goodness. In the context of the community, the widows of the Hellenists were neglected, and seven people with Greek names were chosen to serve at their table. This choice could also inspire our communities when discriminations happen. Why don't we choose a group of women, divorced, LGBTQ people, scientists, environmentalists and listen to their stories and needs, finding ways to include them so that the word of God continues to spread, expand, explore the depth of the human and of the Cosmos?

> We are the way, the truth, and the life,
> where the Universe, Earth, and God
> dream, love, imagine, and create.

Notes

1. John Shelby Spong, *Eternal Life: A New Vision* (New York: HarperOne, 2010).
2. Richard Rohr, *Near Occasions of Grace* (Maryknoll, NY: Orbis, 1993), 96.

Eleventh Sunday in Ordinary Time, Holy Trinity

Exod 34:4b-6, 8-9; 2 Cor 13:11-13; John 3:16-18

After the intensity of Lenten and Easter seasons culminated in Pentecost, we have reentered Ordinary Time, the favorable time where the creative wave of the Spirit can expand, permeate, and leaven our daily experience. This Eleventh Sunday ignites again our heart at the flame of the trinitarian life, the mysterious and transforming dynamism at the heart of the world and of the soul.

Are there better words to enlighten the intimate, participative relation of divine life than those expressed by the Gospel of John? God has so passionately loved this world that God has given God's whole being without reserve in the gift of the beloved Son. God has become powerless for love until death. We discover God as eternally involved in a mutual giving and receiving of love. We perceive ourselves not as separate and abandoned beings, but included in an affectionate relationship with the creative Energy that continues to generate the whole evolving Universe, and has become an enfleshed expression of self-giving bestowal in Jesus. From him we receive the Spirit, the overflowing life that even death cannot extinguish, pulling us forward, toward the newness, the fulfillment of the future.

The all-embracing Mercy has so passionately loved the world. What a light and a joy this good news arouses in our hearts! We contemplate the perennial Source of our beings as an ecstatic, expanding, relational dynamism, the Initiator of a cosmic dance that during billions of years has invited onto the dance floor matter and stars, life and consciousness. And has opened our senses to hear this music and to join this extravagant dance. With the big bang, the exuberance

of divine Energy, particles began to conglomerate in atoms and molecules, in stars, galaxies, and planets, and the music of life burst into
the first community of the cell, and swarms of cells wove organs and
bodies, animals and cities, the quivering connections of our synapsis,
the connecting organs of our eyes and hands, of our feelings. It looks
like God is intensifying this community of life that is our world.

We are an ecological, inter-being web of life. We bring inscribed
in our heart a trinitarian, communicative DNA. How, then, could it
happen that in the name of this relational, triune God, we have hated,
uniformed, hurt, oppressed, polluted, excluded? Today we are largely
embarrassed at the way we have treated people of color, women, the
divorced, LGBTQ people, Jews, and members of religions different
from our own, how greedily we have exploited our planet Earth,
causing extinction and waste. Maybe mistakes, limits and failures,
betrayals, misunderstandings, and inner darkness are a painful part
of birthing the Divine in our story. We dramatically experience that
a part of us wants to exclude and dominate, yet the divine part in us
cannot live without the other, wants to be on the side of those who
suffer, becoming a powerful stimulus to overcome personal, social,
and ecological causes of suffering. The Spirit of the dying and rising
Christ is there, embracing the wider community of life on Earth.

I would like to highlight a further aspect of the triune God as a
self-giving mystery. We have a powerful image in our Sun that
mirrors this mystery. We can be inspired by the spiritual significance
of the Sun. "Five billion years ago the hydrogen atoms, created at the
birth of the universe, came together to form our great Sun that now
pours out this same primordial energy and has done so from the
beginning of time."[1] This gratuitous and ongoing flow of energy
causes the vitality of the Earth and our own vitality, so that we are
able to feel, to thrive, to think, and to create, because flowing through
our bloodlines are molecules energized by the Sun. The Sun's story,
the Sun's bestowal of free energy blossoms in human hearts, in men
and women who feel the urgency to devote their lives to the well-
being of the larger community, so that others might live and thrive.
Prophets, men and women of all times and cultures, witness the
radiation of this expanding mystery of compassion.

Triune God, like a radiating Sun, abides in our hearts: "You ask me
what the human soul is?" Meister Eckhart says. "No human science

can ever fathom what the soul is in its depth. But this we know: The soul is where God works compassion."[2] And in her book *The Interior Castle*, St. Teresa of Avila says that the "soul is vast, spacious, and plentiful. This amplitude is impossible to exaggerate. . . . The sun at the center of this place radiates to every part . . . and nothing can diminish its beauty."[3]

Are we able to participate in a cosmic dance of giving and receiving love? Are we willing to be vessels of solar and trinitarian generosity in our earthly, daily journey of life?

Triune God
dance of love who cannot live
without the other,
welcoming hospitality
that culminates in your crucified embrace.
Your womb guards dark and light,
openness and resistance, joy and cry.
Hope, faith, and Love are your hatching eggs,
yeast of the Earth,
seed of the future.

Notes

1. Brian Swimme, *The Hidden Heart of the Cosmos: Humanity and the New Story* (Maryknoll, NY: Orbis, 1996), 43.

2. Matthew Fox, *Christian Mystics: 365 Readings and Meditations* (Novato, CA: New World Library, 2011), 142.

3. St. Teresa of Avila, *The Interior Castle*, trans. Mirabai Starr (New York: Riverhead, 2003), I, 2.

Fifteenth Sunday in Ordinary Time

Isa 55:10-11; Rom 8:18-23; Matt 13:1-23

A sower went out to sow. This image of a generous and tireless sower reminds me of the beautiful story told by the paleontologist and historian of science Stephen Jay Gould in his book *Wonderful Life: The Burgess Shale and the Nature of History*. The scientific storyteller lets us participate in the fascinating discovery of the Burgess fauna in the western Canadian Rockies, an exceptional site of fossilized invertebrates, where our eyes are opened by how life's creativity and imagination run wild and free. In this fossilized episode of evolution we discover that nature generated a wonderful surplus of organisms with the most fanciful forms, as if Life wanted to explore many possibilities for a short time before totally disappearing, leaving only a few species to exist and to develop. We can be surprised by the same abundant evolutionary activity in the spreading of new living forms from the group of great apes. A great variety of hominids existed on the continents for a long time, until a gifted species, rich with promise, emerged: *Homo sapiens sapiens*, and all the other branches of hominids became extinct.

Let us first contemplate these countless seeds of the Universe, of galaxies, and of our planet Earth as expressions of divine, lavish generosity. Life, the Universe, or God are these excessive and wasteless sowers that continually sow seeds of life regardless of their chances of success or failure, receptivity or adversity, fruitfulness or extinction. Despite the outcomes, life expands, deepens, and inaugurates unexpected and unpredictable ways to evolve. Another source of contemplation and of gratitude springs up when we turn

our gaze to the bountiful seeds of women and men who have contributed to the blossoming of our consciousness, nurturing the seeds
of human feelings, visions, and actions: prophets, healers, inventors,
divergents, thinkers, artists, spiritual and social guides. And among
these multitudes we welcome Jesus as the sower of wisdom and
compassion in our earthly adventure.

Jesus reveals an extreme passion for the world that he expresses
in the many seeds he sows: gestures of empathic listening; healing
of wounds; taking care of the excluded; opening a reign of love where
divisions, powers, and hatred reign; inaugurating new beginnings
for people stuck in guilt, repression, and dominion. He reveals our
unitive link with God, the intimate connection between sower, seed,
and soil. He embodies radical concern and becomes the seed that
dies into the earth to bear fruit. He incarnates the vital truth that if
we want to save our lives we must spend them with abandon, showing us the path of transformation, the gateway into the very being of
God.

A sower went out to sow. The prophet Isaiah compares the rain
and snow that fall and make the earth fertile and fruitful to the word
of God's will that acts and transforms creation and human hearts.
Yet, we experience in nature and in our existence that there is not an
immediate cause and effect. "Before spring becomes beautiful and
the seeds sprout it is plug ugly, nothing but mud and muck."[1] We
learn by experience that, often and paradoxically, in the muddy mess
the conditions for rebirth and resurrection are being created. Humili-
ating events, demise, insecurity, discomfort, and bewildering periods
of our life may create the fertile soil in which something new and
unexpected can surface and grow.

Today, the gospel invites us also to cope with resistances. Resistance is probably one of the greatest barriers to growth. There is a
mystery of not listening, of hardening. There is in us, individually
and as a group, a drive to sabotage, a destructive and divisive force;
there is a refusal or a fear to change. How is it so hard to listen to the
voice that calls us to the fullness of life, to a new level of consciousness, or to a widening of heart?

Maybe we have interiorized voices in our childhood that told us
we were bad, wrong, not enough, unlovable, unworthy, selfish.
Behavior-controlling tactics always suppress life. How can we now

believe in that loving, gentle, and welcoming voice that sees no wrong in us, and pulls us to develop our potential gifts?

Maybe the hidden and powerful economic interests in favor of groups and corporations have made us deaf to the blossoming of justice, inclusion, and sustainability, and resistant to every new insight that menaces our interests. Consider the poor scientists and ecologists who are ringing the alarm bells of an ecological disaster, but too many people are not listening, especially the big oil companies and those with political responsibilities.

The parable of the gospel suggests that a benevolent and generous sower continues to sow seeds of life and compassion, notwithstanding life's adversities. Whenever we allow ourselves to receive, to welcome, to listen, our existences are transformed and life and relationships prosper and blossom.

We all are sowers in our age; what kind of seeds are we sowing? Do we perceive and love our personal seeds and gifts? Do we cultivate them with passion? Do we give them with generosity to others?

> All creation is groaning in labor pains.
> We are God's self unfolding,
> promised seeds planted in time.
> And there is a potential energy of love
> at the heart of every seed,
> asking for receptive ears.
> Inviting us to trust
> in what we don't see yet,
> in this mysterious yeast of grace
> soaring free
> in the skies of our bodies.

Note

1. Parker J. Palmer, *Let Your Life Speak: Listening for the Voice of Vocation* (San Francisco: Jossey-Bass, 2000), 103.

Nineteenth Sunday in Ordinary Time

1 Kgs 19:9a, 11-13a; Rom 9:1-5; Matt 14:22-33

In the present situation of the world we can feel attuned with today's gospel. We are on a boat in a rough sea, a metaphor for personal, communal, and planetary storms. Yet we may be met inside these turbulences by the Incomprehensible, by a Presence that is beyond our forces and control, challenging us in a journey of transforming faith. Perhaps we are invited to contemplate and to welcome this storming and creative Mystery. God can be not as nice as we would like, and in Jesus the divine goes through and rises from the storm of a violent death.

In contrast to the idea of a static Universe, the Cosmos began with a huge, fiery storm. The birthplace of the expanding immensity in which we live started as a great flaring forth from a tiny seed point that was trillions of degrees hot and that instantly rushed apart. For half a million years particles of matter and light churned ceaselessly, colliding and scattering apart millions of times each instant. Then, gradually, the Universe cooled down, and allowed the first atoms to merge.[1]

A multitude of other tempests characterize the nature of our Cosmos: stellar turbulences, supernova explosions, colliding of galaxies. And in our wonderful planet massive upheavals are at the origin of the formation of the Earth's crust. Not to mention the bursting of human storms that we daily experience: tribal, political, religious, racial, gender-related, financial, ecological, and existential.

Some years ago an Israeli director, Eytan Fox, created a movie with the emblematic title *Walk on Water*. In the final scene two men are moving forward on the surface of an Israeli lake. How is it possible that two persons walk on the water? The unbelievable event happens thanks to a troubled and dramatic journey related to the personal and collective story of the two protagonists. One is Jewish, is part of the secret services of the state: he is a machine planned to kill the enemies. The other one is a young German, grandson of a general who had been one of the cruelest persecutors of Jews during Nazism. Both, whether they like it or not, are parts of a story marked by hatred and destructive violence, a surface troubled by overwhelming waters.

However, trying to take steps between doubts and mistrust, between thoughts of revenge and fear of the alien, between illusion of impenetrability and the acceptance of vulnerability, the two will gradually be able to generate a mutual trust, a fraternal and no more fratricidal relationship. Taking upon themselves a story scarred by the wounds of enmity, risking on the waters of an allowed trust, the impossible miracle gushes: the grace to be able to walk on the water.

What prevents this wonder from happening between an Israeli and a Palestinian, or an American and an Iraqi, or humans and their disrupted environment, or us and the hurts or the past memories lodged in our bodies? Perhaps a speck of faith and trust in an embedding Source who loves each one of us?

From the experience of Elijah on the mountain and of Peter on the sea, we learn that the divine comings often astound and undermine our expectations, behaviors, assuring routes. The divine passages are never innocuous or guaranteed—we would like so!—but they instead provoke upheavals in our emotions, consciousness, and actions. A radical overturn happens on the mountain: Elijah is repeatedly deprived of a mighty, revengeful, and judgmental Godhead. His intolerant, religious compulsion to impose his own God on others collapses. He is reconfigured to an unprecedented experience of the Hidden Heart of the world as *a sound of sheer silence*. The all-embracing Abyss wraps itself in silence, blows as a gentle breeze without a "why."

Maybe the God of life gratuitously shines in elusive gestures, glances, shades, touches, luminous intuitions, and in silences imbued with unspoken potentialities. However, we are not mistaken. Silence is not a conclusion but a transformative opening of the future. It becomes a summoning voice: *"Elijah, what are you doing here? Go, return on your way."* And a new mandate and responsibility follows.

Peter also is surprised: Jesus is not a reassuring presence on the boat. Yet very often that is what we want—a God who reflects our culture, our biases, our economic, religious, political, and military systems. Yet, the human-divine comes from afar, from outside the frontier, from the future of love, unexpected and beyond recognition, as it happened to the disciples of Emmaus, to Mary Magdalene, or to Paul on his way to Damascus.

We will not take certainty from this Ghost, we might take heart: *Come on, Peter, come out on the challenging waters of this unfinished Universe!* We learn from Peter that we are never born to life without passing through a crucible of suffering and love, a baptism of trial and doubt, a contamination with negativity and ambiguity, contradiction and paradox. As Richard Rohr invites us, at a certain point of our journey of faith we move from a splitting knowledge to a contemplative wisdom: we are called to embrace life *and* death, divine *and* human, center *and* margins, infinite *and* finite, human *and* non-human, beginnings *and* endings.

How does the God of life and love come forward on the seas of our lives? Acknowledging that the gaze of God shines in the body of Jesus of Nazareth, and in everybody; that we find force in our weakness; that we find faith in the crises of the world; that we find God in the one who broke his body for an excessive passion, arising our faith in the trustworthiness of love.

Take heart, it is I; do not be afraid.

Note

1. Brian Swimme and Thomas Berry, *The Universe Story: From the Primordial Flaring Forth to the Ecozoic Era* (San Francisco: HarperSan Francisco, 1992).

Fourth Sunday of Advent

2 Sam 7:1-5, 8b-12, 14a, 16;
Rom 16:25-27; Luke 1:26-38

In the first episode of the movie *The Lord of the Rings: The Fellowship of the Ring*, a company of nine is about to cross the dangerous Mines of Moria. During this underground crossing the young hobbit Frodo confesses to old Gandalf, "I wish none of this had happened," and the ancient wise one answers, "So do all who live to see such times, but that is not for them to decide. All we have to decide is what to do with the time that is given to us."[1]

All we have to decide is what to do with the time that is given to us. The sound of this sentence resonates in me in a particular way as we are getting closer to the celebration of one of the most beautiful expressions of God's creativity and love in the Universe: the birth, the manifestation of Jesus. Like him, his parents, and his people, we are also living in hard times, and we cannot change the destiny we have been assigned to live, but we can at least decide what to do with the time given to us, according to the personal and collective contexts in which we live.

I believe that the two main characters starring in today's readings, David and Mary, evoke different ways we can commit ourselves. They are like a mirror reflecting us to ourselves. One possible embodiment is that of King David (2 Sam 7:1-16). Settled at last in his house, after the building of his kingdom, he wants a house for God also, but in spite of his good intentions, a prophetic voice rises that contradicts his generous yet controlling project. The desire for *settlement* is certainly one of the strongest drives of our life, under the conditions of contingency, vulnerability, and uncertainty. We also want to ally ourselves with the source of our strength and security. We want to build a house for the One that vouches for our projects and plans. But life, or God's creativity, is beyond our control, because the creative Energy is not limited by our human intentions and convictions and surpasses what we think and are capable of.

"Are you the one to build a house for me to live in? Am I not the guy who has been moving about, incessant source of liberation from slavery and fear, idolatry, dereliction and violence? It is I who will make you a house, will raise up an offspring, and I shall be a Father to you." In this prophetic voice there is still powerfully present the ideal of an exclusive election of a people and of a royal race, to the exclusion of the others. These limitations teach us to accept the pace of the God of evolution, whose presence and action never emerge fully at once but glimmer through the cultural and historical occurrences of our lives, opening us to the unexpected, the incalculable, and the wild.

We are aware today that the Universe is permeated by an astounding creativity that lives in all of us and attunes us to the mysterious ways of God, embracing its unexpected surprises and changes. And one of these unexpected surprises is Mary, an unknown teenager from the obscure village of Nazareth who shows us how an individual decision can bring collective, colossal change. She is in fact chosen to enter a new pathway of exploration and embodiment of the yet unborn intentions of God, who doesn't govern the world with direct and miraculous interventions but emerges in our hearts, urging and supporting us toward a personal response to our historical present.

The angel is that vibration, intuition, impulse that pulls her and us forward, into the openness, with no guarantees beyond trust, beckoning us to courageously leap beyond the small confines of our cultural and religious environment, and to surrender to a plan other than our own. The angel creates in her, as it does in us, a *field of readiness*, an inner, silent, and mindful sanctuary for the birth and the irradiation of the Beloved, showing that every moment is full of potential revelation. With a humble audacity, she consciously aligns herself with the Unknown. Her consent becomes the fertile soil for the birth of Jesus, of a new consciousness of God as Father and Mother of all of us. That makes us brothers and sisters beyond exclusion and discrimination.

If I have named *settlement* the drive of King David, I would like to now call the response of Mary *ecstatic*. I don't mean by this a spiritual journey that calls us beyond the world or away from our time and space, but which opens us to the future *in* our world, a future that is not under our control, and yet makes us responsible, cocreators with the energy, intelligence, and love that we call Divine.

Ecstatic is our God, the most irregular guy of the Universe! But not all unsettling is ecstatic: there can be oppressive unsettling. The financing world of the global capitalism, for example, plays to unsettle the markets and cause poverty and unemployment. The unsettling of the greenhouse gases causes dangerous levels of global warming. An unpredictable bombing can disfigure the face of the world. The sudden Apostolic Visitation of Institutes of Women Religious in the United States was intended to halt a new incarnation and consciousness of religious life. We can welcome as ecstatic that unsettling permeated by care and consolation, surprise and healing. This enables us to grow through our choices, achievements, or even failures, as it has been in the paschal mystery of God's love.

We are close to Christmas. What dispossessions are we ready to accept, which creates a virgin space in us for the emerging God of the Universe? What angels in the current situation of the world do we dare to welcome? Are we grateful to the pulsing Energy that dissolves things already done and prepares us to risk together a future yet undone?

Source of perennial renewal and creation
you make new the world each day,
calling every being to participate in the making of it.
With David, Mary, and all men and women of history
let us be enlightened by the grace of your Son Jesus Christ
who continues to be generated in our hearts
in the political, economic, and spiritual choices
we accomplish every day on the planet Earth
toward a future of hope, justice, and peace.
Amen.

Note

1. *The Lord of the Rings: The Fellowship of the Ring*, directed by Peter Jackson (Los Angeles: New Line Cinema, 2001).

Second Sunday in Ordinary Time

1 Sam 3:3b–10, 19; 1 Cor 6:13c–15a, 17–20; John 1:35–42

They came and saw where he was staying, and they remained with him that day.

After the Christmas season, culminating with the Epiphany and the Baptism of Jesus, we are invited to trace the divine presence in our ordinary time and space. It is still the very same Energy of attraction and transformation that pervades today's evangelical scenario. As the angels, during the night, revealed the Light to the shepherds and the star to the magi, so does John with his disciples. He points out the person for whom he is the foreword, the forerunner, urging them to move forward, beyond himself, to the one "who comes after me" (John 1:15). John invites them to participate in the shifting paradigm of consciousness that shines in Jesus, surpassing their beliefs and convictions. He exposes them to a process of compassion and freedom of unimaginable proportions, changing who they are, transforming them into change-agents, making them vessels of a new creation. Jesus' creative energy, radiating goodness, empathy, and inclusiveness, captivates the disciples' emotions and imagination, so that their journey becomes a participation and a commitment to this new Emergence of Love.

They came and saw where he was staying, and they remained with him that day.

What fascinates us and makes us stay with him? What changes in our relationships, in our personal and social structures because of our connection with Jesus? What is our stay like? Is it routine, an inherited tradition, security, or is it a subtle and unexpected presence that whispers and awakes us, like Samuel, who was sleeping in the temple, and propels us beyond the boundaries of who we are now as persons, communities, and cultures? Like every son and daughter of God, Samuel realizes over time that his very body is the temple of the Holy Spirit present among us, urging us to undertake an unpredictable journey in uncharted territories. I believe that the space of faith we are invited into is not a place where we can settle or control, but rather it is . . . *a flame*! I feel that faith is the transforming flame in our relationship with the divine Energy, which tries to break us free, to release us from the historical weight of our conditioning, both personal and cultural.

Faith as a flame. I have been powerfully impressed by Cormac McCarthy's novel *The Road*, which has also become a motion picture. An apocalyptic event has occurred on the earth. Nature has been destroyed, reduced to a parched, ransacked land. Everything is plunged into a gray atmosphere, saturated with ashes and desolation.

Human beings have become hunters, one against the other, reduced to survival, brutality, and savagery. All the values of civilization, including beauty, goodness, and joy, have been swept away. In this context of absolute desperation, the only spark of meaning and humanity shines in the journey of two people, a father with his son, who are moving south to survive the approaching winter. More essentially, we slowly perceive that they are carrying *the fire* of care and goodness through a world overwhelmed by violence and death. It is this interior fire that the father enkindles in his son. It is the only breath of the passing God. It is the flame of an unshakable, spiritual confidence, in the midst of the unending storm of atrocities, entrusted to the responsibility of human beings.

They came and saw where he was staying, and they remained with him that day.

How do we carry, enhance, and spread the fire, the liberating and loving flame in our contexts of life? What kind of embracing flame are we committed to, for example, in the wonderful and challenging discoveries of technology and science, in the interfaith dialogue, in the care for the planet, in respect to the laws of a country that tries to create a fair and equitable society?

You now breathe, O God, within each of us,
and among us as a greater capacity of love.
The stretched arms on the cross are measures of your compassion:
broken walls of inclusion, blossoming of peace in every heart.
You enter the world, O God, through us:
through our courage to live life hopefully each day,
through our passion to endlessly love,
and to make every moment that is given to us
a particle of your eternity.

Year B

First Sunday of Lent
Gen 9:8-15; 1 Pet 3:18-22; Mark 1:12-15

On Friday morning a maintenance worker came to inspect the furnaces of our monastery, to clean the filters and the vents, to lubricate the moving parts of the heating system. Since Ash Wednesday we have also embarked on a journey of cleaning and lubrication of the mechanisms of our personal and collective visions, choices, and goals.

The Lenten season can in fact turn out to be an opportunity for all of us to become more connected to and focused on the furnace that moves, warms, and refreshes our Christian experience, namely, the paschal mystery. Easter is indeed the pulsing heart of our Lent—the good news that God is not settled in his own completion but is emerging in a wild and unruly Universe, participating in the human suffering, in the process of a new creation.

God shines in the body of Jesus of Nazareth. In Jesus he establishes a new relatedness, so deep a connection with humanity that even the overwhelming strength of evil and hatred cannot erase. God's immediacy responds to Jesus' radical self-giving, by raising him from the dead. The personal and collective rite of passage that we are about to enter reminds us that resurrection, the creative and immanent newness of God, is waiting to unfold in our bodies. Our personal and social bodies are the places where God is arising, doing unprecedented things. After reminding ourselves of this deep thread that connects the Lenten season with Easter, let us move closer to today's readings.

The gospel helps us to identify the Agent and Instigator of our transformative journey. *The Spirit drove Jesus out into the wilderness* (Mark 1:12). Tricky is the Spirit, isn't she? She drives us out into the wilderness. She is neither a Spirit of accommodation, or mere survival, nor a comfortable companion. She is rather a driving, unsettling force that makes us embark on a journey with openness, risk, and uncertainty. She causes unexpected shifts and transitions and leaps to new levels of freedom, love, and responsibility.

From the very beginning, the Spirit is driving out the Universe into the wilderness. She is the propelling energy that ignites the fire of life, flares forth into the newness of unexplored spaces. This journey is also a passage through collapses that allow the renewal of life, such as the one described in the first reading. From the devastating flood emerges a new consciousness and relationship among God, humans, and planet Earth.

Like Noah, we also can experience the fact that an entire setup of values and structures is falling apart. We can be tempted to prop up the existent system of exploitation, pollution, and war, or to fully accept the enormity of this exodus with all the uncertainty, risk, disorientation, deep grief, and even horror that it will entail. The death of our cultural identity can in fact represent the opportunity for a spiritual transition through which the limitations and mistakes of our immature worldview can be purged and transfigured. And maybe, from the depths of this enormous process, from the baptism through death, a new humanity and a new image of God are arising.

The Spirit is in fact challenging us to cast off our *egocentric* ways of living, and to surrender to a new *ecocentric* awareness. What does it mean? It means that we are no more the undisputed rulers of the world, but we belong to the bigger story of the Universe; we owe what we are to all the living beings that surround us. Following in the footsteps of Jesus we learn to live in the company of the Spirit, the beasts, the demons, and the angels.

Jesus incarnates the passion of an inclusive embrace of all the creatures, including the demons that populate the depths of the human soul, with whom he starts a healing dialogue. Jesus is driven out by Love into the wilderness in a *crescendo* of clarity, passion, and participation. He breaks into, and through, our personal, religious, and social structures, our frames of dominion, violence, and exclusion. He opens people's eyes, ears, and hearts to allow God to thrive and renew our ways of living on Earth together.

As does every person guided by the Spirit, Jesus meets resistance and persecution. Suffering, pain, and death are indeed part of the journey of the Universe, part of the passion of God, who participates in the labor of an ever-deepening love.

At the beginning of this Lenten season, we open our hearts to the trustworthy good news that God's compassion is stronger than all our deaths, and she is creative! We commit ourselves to the invisible, effective thread of God's love.

I offer you as traveling companion of this liturgical season a poem of William Stafford, "The Way It Is":[1]

> There's a thread you follow. It goes among
> things that change. But it doesn't change.
> People wonder about what you are pursuing.
> You have to explain about the thread.
> But it is hard for others to see.
> While you hold it you can't get lost.
> Tragedies happen; people get hurt
> or die; and you suffer and get old.
> Nothing you do can stop time's unfolding.
> You don't ever let go of the thread.

Note

1. William Stafford, "The Way It Is," in *The Way It Is: New and Selected Poems* (Minneapolis: Graywolf, 1998), 42.

Second Sunday of Lent

Gen 22:1-2, 9a, 10-13, 15-18;
Rom 8:31b-34; Mark 9:2-10

Some years ago, a now well-known African American by the name Mr. Barack Obama was inspired by a luminous vision for his election campaign, coining a slogan that echoed throughout his nation and the world . . . and allowed him to win! "We can change. Yes, we can!" or, in other words, we can draw energy from a reliable source within us, which permits us to turn what seems to be an irreversible condition of discontent into something new, different, shared.

I find that the possibility to modify, to renew, to transcend the "given" of our personal and community lives is the core of our experience of *transfiguration*, the discovery that what we call matter, reality, fact, body, or self are not just fixed identities but are expressions of the enormous flux of becoming in which everything is figured, disfigured, and refigured. Reality is a flow in which we are immersed, empowered to forge and to develop our personal self, to become available to the unfolding of the invisible in our personal, social, and global body.

Let us first be surprised by the innumerable *changes* that have allowed us to become something else that we were not at the beginning. Let us be first amazed at what the Cosmos has become, from the big bang to now. What the globalized world has become, from separateness to connectedness. We contemplate the beauty, the promise of becoming, but also the challenges, the pangs, the wounds, the dark nights that have generated what we are at present, our relationships, our faith.

I desire to evoke some events that may be considered favorable spaces for a transfiguration, in the mountains or in the deserts of our daily life, like an enlarging spiral of the divine that incarnates itself in the eternal restlessness of becoming.

The *first* hint of transfiguration I desire to evoke is *the charm of creativity*. I acknowledge that I am the word that God has assigned to me to embody in the world: "You are my son and daughter, the beloved." I can love and accept myself. I can develop the gifts that I have received, embrace the lights and shades, the known and the unknown that surround myself. I can give shape to the future and welcome it. I am invited to become father and mother of new life. I can open to the spiritual dynamism that inspires and illuminates me. I discover myself sustained by a spirit that protects me and spurs me forward, relating and celebrating with others the joy and the pain of life: that is the meaning that we are here, gathered together in this Eucharist, to open ourselves to the Source of every transformation, urging us to strengthen our communion and trust.

I recognize a *second* transfiguring event in *the compassionate glance*, when my self-centered or indifferent look toward the other turns into something different. When I begin to notice the presence, the weight, the gift, the pain of the other, what shines or moans in the eyes of the person I meet, letting fall the frozen walls of division to foreshadow something more, deeper, yearning for meaning or for joy. Saints, wise men and women of all time and cultures, are the embodiment of this compassionate glance, in the same wave of the Spirit of Jesus, who tried to free from impediments the bodies of the persons he met, to let the divine light blossom freely through them.

Finally, I perceive a *third* movement of transfiguration in *the ecological awareness*. There is not only "I" and "we," but we are interconnected and involved in a web of life that we are discovering more and more in all its expressions as Cosmos and biosphere, as waters and plants and animals. At the same moment we are trying to unite minds around the world in a global, telematics space, forged by the convergence of computers and telecommunications. Are we invigorating divisive oppositions or are we consenting to the divine energy to release connections among natural, social, cultural, technological currents that make life on this planet possible?

This critical juncture requires risking a faith that embraces uncertainty and insecurity as conditions of creative emergence. These three challenges invite us to connect ourselves to the open Source of love that presses at the borders of our singularity to open it, indefinitely, to what it has not yet been born.

I end with a hint of Etty Hillesum's diaries, written in the concentration camp where she was confined, offering a new image of the connection between God and each one of us: "One thing is becoming increasingly clear to me: that You cannot help us, that we must help You to help ourselves . . . that we safeguard that little piece of You, God, in ourselves. . . . You cannot help us, but we must help You and defend Your dwelling place inside us to the last."[1]

Note

1. Etty Hillesum, *An Interrupted Life* (New York: Henry Holt, 1996), 178.

Easter Vigil

Rom 6:3-11; Mark 16:1-7

To what feast, to what celebration are we invited tonight? We are lit up with exultation by God's liberating and destabilizing action. Tonight our hearts greatly rejoice at the good news that the divine Energy is a caring presence that transforms *death into new life*—in the Universe, in our world, in our relationships, in the deep parts of our bodies.

On Friday, Jesus plunged us down into a deep night of despair because of his violent end and burial. With him all our hopes, trusts, struggles, and yearnings sank into an impenetrable silence. We must face the tomb, the disintegration of all understanding and explanation. How do we make sense of this incomprehensible event in our human experience? Yet, at the core of this abysmal horror that can crack open at any moment during our lives, in our neighborhoods or in our country, an unexpected earthquake happens, a big bang of grace that creates life out of death. In the abyss of Jesus' death, God's Spirit is still present, hovering upon the chaos, creating something new and unexpected, beyond anything we can conceive of in our minds. In the deep and terrible nights of our world, gripped by violence, greed, dominion, security's obsessions, and exclusion, the creative Breath full of potentialities is opening us, freeing us to a future of greater generosity, equality, peace, caring for everyone and for the planet Earth.

The stories that accompany the unfolding of this sacred night tell us of the many and amazing events in which death is integral to the processes of life, and allows the transformation in new life. Genesis, exodus, exile, Easter . . . all these dramatic and glorious mysteries reveal to us that the ever-new creation of God is emerging from within many forms of suffering as part of a birthing process toward a richer life, a surprising future.

The fourteen billion years of evolutionary history have been made possible because of death and the emergence of always new life. Exodus, likewise, has been a risky and mortal journey through a stripping desert, giving up the old securities and survival patterns toward a promised, unknown land.

In this holy night of Christ's resurrection, God emerges as a mystery of relatedness and self-giving love. Pushed out of the world, weak and powerless, he embraces death and self-emptying. Assuming our vulnerability and continuing to love, he shows us to be the God-with-us. Being all interconnected, in the grand adventure of evolution, Jesus' transformation of death in life has profound consequences on the whole of creation, far beyond him. Jesus inaugurates a kingdom of grace, showing that God is present in history, not because of sin but because of his passionate love for the world, for every sentient being. A radical love that dissolves the barriers we continually raise in defense of our excluding egos, cultures, or religions with their ramifications of mortal conflicts and exclusions.

Jesus awakens the depths of our human and cosmic evolution. He empowers creatures to do new things. Discovering ourselves as part of the liberation story of the Universe, as part of the divine transformations, something truly miraculous begins to happen in us. We are, in fact, the continuation of Christ in everyday life, God's indwelling vessel. The direction of evolution begins to depend on our choices, imagination, action, hope, beyond our needs to control, dominate, and waste the world.

Tonight we are grateful to God's trinitarian Love,
pulsing heart of the Universe.
Embracing the world with unconditional compassion,
Christ embraces the vulnerability of every life.
Assuming suffering he transforms it from within,
from self-concern to self-giving,
toward greater depths of love, hope, and future.
Alleluia!

Year B

Fourth Sunday of Easter
Acts 4:8-12; 1 John 3:1-2; John 10:11-18

Let us first pause with reverence before this ancient figure of the Shepherd, so universally present in rural cultures for thousands of years. From Homer's *Odyssey* to *Brokeback Mountain*, literature of the world tells us stories of shepherds and flocks.

In the Bible, God too is depicted as a compassionate Shepherd, leading Israel toward green pastures and viable paths. The metaphor of the shepherd has also been attributed to the *pastors* of the Israelites. Their service has been called *pastoral*, yet their hunt for abused power attracts the invectives of God. A contagious virus that has not yet been extinguished!

In the middle of our Easter journey, the Gospel of John invites us to contemplate an image of Jesus as a marginalized Jewish peasant who was killed by the Pious and the Powerful. Yet he has become for us a trustful *Good Shepherd*, inviting us to align with him as the compassionate Guide in the here and now of our personal, communal, and planetary journey. I feel it is extremely important for us to dwell upon the salient features that characterize this good, scandalous, and subversive Shepherd. In fact, these traits display the *qualities* of our relationship to God, to our fellow beings, and to the planet.

The three peculiar qualities of Jesus as a Shepherd point out that *he takes care of the sheep; he leads them out; he has to pay attention to other sheep that do not belong to this fold.*

He takes care of the sheep. The first and main trait of Jesus' existence consists *in his taking care* of the boundless aspects in which life manifests herself. When we are insensitive, careless, and absentminded in our daily life, blinded by our rules, habits, or fears, Jesus opens our senses to see, to listen, to touch, and to voice our feelings. *He* has senses and opens *our* senses. He *is* utmost attention, able to ignite the invisible in the texture of our journey. Revealing a divine and creative aptitude, Jesus embraces the inexhaustible treasures that every moment offers to us. With exquisite tact he detects and unravels the shameful or oppressive sides of our hearts; the stiffness and closeness of our personal and social bodies; the unnamable wounds of our hearts . . . and he heals, opens, transforms them! He carries to the extreme his sensibility to include his tormentors in his love, and the last enemy—death. His care is so deep and radical that he goes so far as to lay down his life for the sheep, so wonderfully expressed in the context of the Last Supper: "Having loved his own who were in the world, he loved them to the end" (John 13:1). Do our personal lives, communities, and societies follow Jesus, growing in care, health care, mindfulness, and heartfulness? Or do we anesthetize the sensuous God in our small and manageable moral, logical, social, and religious systems? Are we able to recognize God in the specific glances, voices, and pains of our fellow humans and nonhumans, or are we just enacting regulations and principles that are universal and abstract, emptied of divine pathos, passion, and inspiration?

He leads them out. Where is the resurrected and cosmic Christ leading us? Out from where? To what pastures, to what new life is he taking us today? The Good Shepherd is guiding humanity to a breakthrough in consciousness that can no longer sustain the myth of God as separate somewhere above, or the story of the original Fall as a reason for the coming of Christ. Our communities cannot thrive with an all-male, controlling hierarchy that claims for itself religious liberty but at the same time is ready to curtail the freedom, faith, and courage of the Leadership Conference of Women Religious. The Good Shepherd is guiding us out of closed and self-protected systems, toward open fields of consciousness that include women on all levels of life, toward a land of equal opportunities for gays, lesbians, bisexuals, and transsexuals. He is guiding us toward a territory of participation, of care for the Earth, of creative encounters among religions, of a new technological collective awareness.

He has to pay attention to other sheep. The third aspect that marks Jesus as a Good Shepherd is that *he has to pay attention to other sheep that do not belong to this fold.* We realize with joy that because we are evolving, we are not yet complete. God himself and Christ are in evolution. Christians, churches, believers, religions, cultures are no more identified by their belonging to a single, exclusive tribe but discover themselves in a mutual interrelatedness. Beyond the rigid labels and the folds that have protected and fixed us until now, and that we would like to never change, we are participating in a new era and energy that involves spiritual seekers from everywhere, following the Good Shepherd of compassionate inclusiveness, cooperation, healing, pluralism, and interconnection. The Shepherd binds different peoples to one another and the earth in oneness of heart, opening doors and windows of uncharted territories.

Is he beckoning us from beyond the limited and narrow confines where we are living toward the greater heart of God? Is he initiating a chain of events beyond our control, awakening us to hope and joy beyond discouragement?

Jesus, good shepherd, guide, and pastor,
open gateway to Infinite love;
You are foreshadowed in every star
that guides the course of sailing and of desire.
You shine
in every initiatory journey
to the sacred heart of consciousness and self,
in every action of liberation from oppression.
Guide our lives and communities
to green meadows,
beyond undisturbed lifestyles of convenience
into the transformative,
fiery experience of your Spirit.
Amen.

Pentecost

Acts 2:1-11; Gal 5:16-25; John 20:19-23

A bewildering question arises among the crowd gathered in Jerusalem for the feast of Pentecost that in the Jewish tradition celebrates the giving of the Torah in the desert: "How is it that each of us hears them speaking in our own native language about God's deeds of freedom, love, and transformation?" (see Acts 2:8-11).

I would like to celebrate the event of the Pentecost as the irradiation of the divine Energy dwelling upon these multiple and fiery tongues that manifest the irreducible and brimming riches of God's mystery in everything that exists. Perhaps it is the generative characteristic of the Spirit to express the invisible action of the God of life through the multifarious manifestations of our bodily languages: the visible, the audible, the palatable, the touchable, and the imaginative. A creative Action that shines at a certain moment in the incarnation of Jesus, God made flesh, and spreads out in the whole of life. The elusive and subtle presence of the Spirit is often evoked by fleeting elements like breath, wind, and flight; water, wine, and fire; music, dance, bits and bytes. . . . She radiates in the inflections of our languages, cultures, spiritual traditions, sciences, and arts. She flashes in the uniqueness of a glance, a gesture, an excited tone of the voice of each one of us, whose mystery is hidden in the depths of God. The Spirit of God improvises, like jazz, being the most creative and effective agent of upheaval and transformation in the world.

The Bible seems to be the most striking example of an inspired epic that embraces countless stories—a poem of improvisations and differences. It embraces the genesis and the last, future horizon of time; tragic and comic events; styles and destinies; struggles, agreements, and misunderstandings; promises, successes, and breakdowns

. . . and in all these tangled stories a Presence unravels, inspires, drives, challenges, moves forward, inward, until it becomes flesh. And what to say of the narratives of religions and cultures, each one expressing what is valuable, meaningful, orienting, and beautiful for the human journey? Are not all of them parts, scores, variations, threads of this immense adventure of Life and of Spirit?

The astonishment of the crowd at Jerusalem witnessing God's wonderful deeds resounds in the wonder of scientists, facing the surprising creativity of the Universe. Trying to tell the story of the Universe's development through time, they discover that the Cosmos arose with a titanic expansion to the rate that enabled life to emerge. According to the new vision of *emergence*, cosmic, natural, and cultural history reveal the permanent generation of new structures and organisms that are not reducible to what came before, although they are continuous with it. Emergence is irreducible novelty, appearance of unanticipated properties, as if the Spirit would permanently be the source of unknown, unpredictable manifestations.

And is not Jesus an unprecedented emergence of the Spirit's creativity and imagination? With him a power of newness comes into a human person, a new inventiveness that is divine and human at once. The fiery tongue of Jesus manifests in the amazing creation of parables, stories, images, and gestures that cause a profound shift in our hearts and minds and inaugurate the *kingdom of God*. Far from dominion, this kingdom of the Spirit brings a new consciousness, speaks *the inclusive language of love* that bursts out in the Universe, and makes us free from the law, from the old patterns of aggression, violence, discrimination, and greed that destroy human relatedness and our planet.

We recognize in Jesus the immediacy of God's presence, the inner pressure of love at the heart of the Universe, and how this passion unites and circulates in a multitude of people, from the Buddha to Gandhi, to Martin Luther King Jr., including the flood of anonymous lovers, creators, and innovators that every day renew the face of the Earth and offer new visions of the world. Yet we know, by experience, that every change is not harmless. It is never truly without emotional scar tissue. A different worldview disturbs and upsets the previous setup. Transformation comes at a great cost, loss . . . and chaos! It demands courage and faith. We give up the old understanding and behavior, and we feel lost. We struggle with inner and outer resistances, consenting to what we don't know and yet urges and presses us. And something greater than us happens and opens. Fears dissolve, and a new freedom shines. A new future enters and unravels.

What are the languages, the fiery tongues we activate today, to make God come alive, to resurrect from the tombs? There are still so many boundaries of intolerance, race, gender, injustice to get over that hinder God's new creation. There is still a need to renew an isolated church that has lost the mordant, the yeast, and the spirit of the gospel. Instead of being in the forefront, she is retiring with fright and aggression into the temple of her self-preservation and defense.

The effusion of the Spirit that we celebrate today may revive *the dangerous memory of Jesus of Nazareth* in whom God has done great deeds, subverting the powers of evil and death, in a renewing act of creation. In Christ's Spirit we participate in the birth of God within, we are opened to his future. We respond with our hope, faith, and love to his improvisations, to what has not yet appeared yet is waiting to emerge. Let us celebrate with a prayer inspired by R.-M. Rilke.

You must know that God
blows in you as a wind
from the beginning.
And if your heart glows
and is not veiled
inside God is acting,
opening, laboring
and enjoying.

Sixteenth Sunday in Ordinary Time

Jer 23:1-6; Eph 2:13-18; Mark 6:30-34

In 2013 the scientific community had the chance to celebrate the presumed discovery of a subatomic particle whose existence was envisaged approximately fifty years ago. The particle in question appears to be the *Higgs Boson*, a peculiar, elusive particle that *gives mass* to the particles of an atom, allowing them to unite in stable relationships that are at the origin of the intricacy and beauty of a dragonfly, of a lilac, of a symphony, of the same sophisticated machine that has originated this scientific discovery, the Large Hadron Collider. From its very beginning our Universe has been permeated by this diffuse, uniform, and *collecting energy* that explains how particles are pulled together in greater, complex, emerging creations and communities; without its unifying force there would be no matter, no Universe, no life, no humans!

This scientific finding ushers us into the still mysterious, deep, and unknown fabric of the Cosmos to which we belong. I ponder the reverberations of this connecting particle at the level of our daily life, of our spiritual journey. Is it not the same unifying stream that we try to pursue in our existence, in our desires, choices, and passions? Is it not that same wholeness and integration of life that we are longing for, always threatened by scattering, bewilderment, and disintegration? Even when we are engaged with passion, care, and commitment in our daily tasks we are always exposed to the frantic pace of our world that causes us to feel broken up, to be out of focus, without purpose, separate and abandoned.

It is precisely in *these* situations of disconnection and exhaustion that the opposite polarity often peeps out, compelling us to connect to the deeper dimensions of our internal Universe, to link up with the source of the creative, healing, and reconciling Energy, *a wholeness of which each of us is a particle and a manifestation.*

In the wonderful and dramatic movie *Beasts of the Southern Wild*, set in the Mississippi Delta of south Louisiana, the world emerges through the lively imagination of a little black girl named Hush-puppy. Exposed to a fluctuating reality of enchantment and dereliction, wilderness and intimacy, delight and devastation, she expresses her deep wisdom of life: "The entire Universe depends on everything fitting together just right" and "if you can fix the broken piece, everything can go right back."[1] Again, out of the infinity of pieces, in the uncertainty and vulnerability of life, a visceral need and desire move us to achieve integration, beauty, fullness, relatedness, and participation.

Jesus invites his exhausted friends and disciples to come away from the frenzied activity of their preaching, healing, and worrying to a deserted place, all by themselves, and rest awhile. He summons them to renew and regenerate in the ceaseless reservoir of energy and compassion that is the throbbing, divine Heart of the Universe: the space of latent potentialities, freedom, and regeneration, but also of subversive and transforming forces.

We receive the invitation to create our personal and communal sacred spaces, silent and receptive spaces that help us *touch the Eternal in ourselves and in others.* All of us have these places, maybe in our minds and hearts, to which we retreat, and from which we gather strength, resilience, and hope to confront the harshness of daily existence. We also create together nourishing places that sustain and enhance the interconnection among different people, and nurture the bonds of a larger communion.

Gathered together in *this* eucharistic space, we recognize in Jesus our *unitive source* to the God of the Universes and of the many sacred names. In his life he manifests the good news of God's healing love, the binding of wounds and of the broken pieces of our personal and social bodies. He embraces in the cross every broken heart. With his resurrection he symbolizes *the divine unbroken wholeness of love.* He breaks down the dividing walls, the hostilities within and between us, and creates in himself *one new creation*, having all access in one Spirit to the Father (Eph 2:14-18). He is the *inconvenient love* in the face of every normative, fixating power of economy, war, religion, race, and gender; *unconventional love* beyond the law with its commandments and ordinances, featuring grace, gratuity, and liberation.

Our epoch is torn apart by destructive oppositions, and our church is building impassable walls in front of the most important issues of our contemporary world. Will we respond to the invitation of the Universe and of the gospel to favor wholeness and relatedness, accepting the uncertainty and the unknown of the journey, trusting in the driving inspiration of God? Let us pray with an excerpt from a poem by Galway Kinnell, "Astonishment":[2]

> On the mountain tonight the full moon
> faces the full sun. Now could be the moment
> when we fall apart or we become whole.
> Our time seems to be up—I think I even hear it stopping.
> Then why have we kept up the singing for so long?
> Because that's the sort of determined creature we are.
> Before us, our first task is to astonish,
> and then, harder by far, to be astonished.

Notes

1. *Beasts of the Southern Wild*, directed by Benh Zeitlin (New Orleans: Court 13 Films, 2012).

2. Galway Kinnell, "Astonishment," *The New Yorker* (July 23, 2012), http://www.newyorker.com/magazine/2012/07/23/astonishment.

Twenty-Second Sunday in Ordinary Time

Deut 4:1-2, 6-8; Jas 1:17-18, 21b-22, 27; Mark 7:1-8, 14-15, 21-23

Having grown used to being stuffed with uncountable trailers before seeing an eagerly awaited movie, I was struck by a funny and significant clip. While a voice tells the audience that our history is woven of events, heroes, adventures, dramas, and comedies that flavor our lives, we taste in wide-screen some of these breathtaking and engrossing scenes of love, war, and freedom. We moviegoers are then taken by surprise to see the same events happening on smaller and smaller screens—from the giant movie screen to the microscreen of a mobile phone—until it is hardly possible to see what is going on. And while the narrative voice complains about this intolerable *reduction* of the riches of life, a sudden *explosion* of the smallest screen occurs, sort of an act of rebellion from life itself that refuses to be sacrificed and almost buried in a too-small technological grave that cannot contain her.

While meditating on the readings of this Sunday, I felt this same complaint burst forth, affirming the irreducibility of all manifestations of life to fixed, narrow, imposed containers. Maybe these rules, patterns, and laws were constructed in the past for good purposes, but are they still serving and enhancing the life that they want to spread? From the beginning, and at every moment of her unpredictable adventure, the creative and loving Energy has experienced herself flaring forth through innumerable inventions and upheavals in the Universe—as planets, sentient and human beings, cultures and religions, our consciousness, emotions, relationships, interactions. The

God of life is permanently generating this immeasurable and challenging novelty, transmutation, and experimentation. How can we stop the process? How can we confine the overflowing Fountain into the boxes of our concepts, definitions, rules, or laws?

The Bible itself witnesses this perennial and unconcluded Genesis of the world, the always unexpected, trustworthy, and risky revelation of the God of exodus and exile, destruction and renewal, chaos and generation. The first reading from Deuteronomy deals with the gift of the Mosaic Law but reinterprets and renews it in the light of later historical experience. Israel walks no more in the desert but is now settled in Canaan. Yet Israel is always attracted by the carved idols of the peoples that surround him, tempted to create a god according to his own measure and use, instead of witnessing with his life a trustworthy relationship to the unnamable Giver of the covenant, one that promotes compassion and justice among the people.

In his journey, Jesus also experiences and confronts the religious constraints of his time, manifesting the compassionate God that inspires and nourishes him. He suffers the hostility of specific groups of people who try to deny or avoid the change and upheaval of life. Among them there are those who are *wealthy*, filled with their own goods, without care for others or for other dimensions of being; there are those who are *religious*, carefully engineering their own willpower, perfection, and superiority systems; and there are those who consider themselves *intelligent*, pretending to reduce the world to the measure of their own understanding.

In one of his songs, the black songwriter Frank Ocean sings, "If it brings me to my knees, it's a bad religion." Jesus doesn't make people bend but rather unbends the people he meets, freeing them from the obstacles or fears that imprison their existence. He awakens latent potentialities, dormant powers. Without dominion and imposition he offers a gratuitous, welcoming space that embraces vulnerability, uncertainty, suffering, and possible resurrections. He shows a revolutionary way to trust and to surrender to Someone deeper and larger than us, in whom we can fall in love. He witnesses this powerful appeal to the Source of compassion in his pining embrace from the cross.

By pulling down every wall of separation that we continually build, Jesus purifies all things. Nothing defiles outside of us, but all dualisms and separations, marginalization and contempt come from within our personal hearts and minds, or within the heart of our cultures, religions, and societies.

Today we experience the crisis and demise of a world that resists and opposes the birth of something fresh with its paralyzing set of tribal structures, behaviors, and rules that are attributed to tradition or to God—and are identified with the truth. We question old understandings because a transformation is breaking through, dismantling our previous conditioning. The apostle James invites us to become *agents* of change, to become *doers* of the wor(l)d and not hearers only. Isn't our individual and collective response to offer our bodies to this new life, with responsibility, care, and faith?

With our bodies we expose ourselves to the subtle and creative breeze of God, aware of a Mystery, open and receptive to others, cultivating a language of interiority, experience, and empathy. We live at the threshold of our time without a fixed, guaranteed abode. We are cooperative with the Spirit in opening the cages and the tombs of the world. We feel reverence for the Earth as conscious parts of her body. We welcome discontinuities, weakness, crises, and even death, with the hope of resurrection, of God's transforming love.

Twenty-Sixth Sunday in Ordinary Time

Num 11:25-29; Jas 5:1-6; Mark 9:38-43, 45, 47-48

While listening to the gospel, we may feel that entering into the kingdom is a bloody slaughter! We wonder what it means that we have to get rid of something in order to enter the kingdom! Let us be introduced to this game of loss and gain by two different stories.

Johannes Kepler, the German astronomer of the sixteenth century, was trying to detect the planetary orbit of Mars, but he was not able to match his theory with what he observed. The venerable and long tradition before him assumed that the planets were moving in circular paths, because the circle was thought to be the perfect, incorruptible, heavenly shape, essentially different from our earthly turmoil, corruption, and change.

The detailed observations of the apparent motion of the planets forced him to realize that the planets were material objects, made of imperfect stuff like our planet Earth, plus their orbits also were irregular. After months of desperation, he figured out that planets travel in *ellipses*. He had to sacrifice his fascination with the perfection of the circle and assume the *sacred imperfection* of the ellipse!

Now, another story of resistance, loss, and revelation. In the Acts of the Apostles (Acts 10), Peter is praying on the roof of the house of his hosts. At this moment of his journey he is orbiting in a circular way around the villages of Judea to visit people to whom he has already announced the Gospel, sharing the same language, customs, behaviors, and religious identity. In this comfort zone there is no initiative, creativity, or risk! While he is praying, however, he experiences *a divine intrusion* that messes up the order of his existence. The heaven opens, and something like a large sheet comes down, a hodge-podge of all kinds of four-footed creatures, reptiles, and birds. And a voice presses Peter to get up, to kill, and to eat.

As Kepler was fascinated with his beloved circle, so Peter is caught in the unchanging perfection of his religious tradition. Startled out of his wits by the voice from above, he opposes with a resolute refusal to change: "Damn it! I have never eaten anything that is profane and unclean." But the subversive answer from on high opens a radical new vision and sensitivity on earth: "What God has made clean, you must not call profane" (Acts 10:15).

Immediately after this event, Peter is asked to incarnate the vision: agents sent from Cornelius, a pagan centurion from Caesarea, arrive and invite Peter to leave and to be a guest at the centurion's house. Peter is urged to enter into contact with people excluded by the law: foreigners, strangers, aliens.

In Peter's enlarged embrace a *loss* happens, the dissolution of a limit that prevented him from stepping forward, stretching out, and welcoming what was repudiated. In his gesture of inclusion he opens a *window of creativity* where the Spirit spreads over and includes the excluded, with great astonishment of everybody.

"Would that all the Lord's *people were prophets, and that the* Lord *would put his spirit on them!"* (Num 11:29).

It is said that human transformation was the only miracle that the Buddha recognized as such. Kepler's and Peter's stories reflect our personal and collective stories of transformation, happening through our losses, perilous times, and new beginnings!

Maybe God's kingdom unexpectedly happens in the narrow and disquieting passages of our life when a voice, a vision, or an event breaks into and upsets the limits of our previous perception and urges us to welcome another way of sensing, envisioning, or acting. Pieces of our previous experience dissolve under the pressure of something new and unknown that is about to be generated in our hearts, if we say yes to the challenge, the risk, and the involvement! God's energy and care don't remain in a separate and perfect sphere but from the beginning flare forth as a creative wave, inspire the hearts of men and women through all the ages, and in an astounding way shine in Jesus, embracing vulnerability, brokenness, and the unknown.

Jesus' life, passion, and death incarnate God's foolish love that overcomes our resistances of control and oppression, arrogance and power, inaugurating a new realm of radical inclusivity, of peace and freedom, of communication and joy. We are pressured from within by Jesus' Spirit to become *channels of God's creativity*, aware that every conscious act, gesture, and decision opens new possibilities and resonates in the atmosphere around us, giving shape to a new world.

What could be the limitations that we are invited or even urged to overcome in our time, to allow the expansion of God's love/kingdom? What can we leave behind, to allow the emergence of a new creation?

We can leave behind the mistrust of God's separation and become aware of God's concern, God's sensuous mystery, breathing in ourselves and in the entire Universe. We can leave behind the fear that the other, as different from ourselves, is a menace for us, thus extinguishing useless wars before they begin. We can dismiss the consumptive drive of our developed world that sacrifices everything to economic growth and enter into a dialogue with the larger Earth community, with all the geological, biological, and human components. We can release religious violence and hierarchical powers that imagine God as an instrument of dominion and exclusion that we possess, and instead foster communities of peace, reverence, mutual creativity, and joy: *"Whoever is not against us is for us"* (Mark 9:40).

You have become flesh, God.
You are the flesh of the world.
Help us to embrace the foolishness of your love wiser
than human wisdom,
to be expansions of your imagination that resurrects us
from our tombs of violence and inhumanity.

Thirty-First Sunday in Ordinary Time

Deut 6:2-6; Heb 7:23-28; Mark 12:28b-34

How have the amazing adventures of *loving relationships* we have heard from the readings unfolded as a commandment in Israel, an embodiment in Christ, a hope for the entire world? Maybe the loving connections began from the first moments of the newborn Universe, when a chaos of frenzied and disconnected particles was pulled together by a spirit of bonding and attraction. Churning and repulsive particles gradually began to relate to each other. It was, at first, a tiny community of atoms. Then several atoms gathered together to form a more instrumental orchestra: a molecule. Then, in an astonishing way, a mantle, a membrane was created, capable of embracing different molecules, and the extraordinary creativity of the cell began to expand and resonate. Choruses of cells composed plants, living organisms, the neural and effervescent community of our brains, together with the complex symphonies of cultures, languages, rituals, and technologies.

We contemplate with awe this exuberance of wider, deeper relationships and connections of life. We acknowledge with reverence the vibrant presence of a divine Eros that radiates through all the networks of the Universe, Earth, bodies, and expanding communities of all spaces and times.

But let us hear now a more dramatic note! When I first saw the movie *The Tree of Life* I was particularly struck by a scene. A walking dinosaur passes by an infant animal and makes the accustomed gesture of stretching its leg above the baby to crush it. Something unexpected, however, happens. The big animal seems to ponder, to hesitate. Touched by grace, so to speak, the dinosaur suddenly takes back its leg and walks forward, sparing the young, defenseless life. This scene suggests that at a certain moment of evolution a miraculous possibility emerged in the world: the possibility for a living being to limit its power or instinct of destruction, and to transform these impulses to create a space of respect for otherness, heralding new relational qualities inspired by care and empathy.

Let us move now from cells and animals into the habitat of humans! On one of the mountains in the land of Moriah, Abraham has prepared an altar to offer to God his firstborn, Isaac (Gen 22). Yet, something surprising happens: he hesitates and stops. We recognize Abraham as the father of believers not because of his willingness to carry out the violent and bloody act of sacrificing his beloved son, but rather because he was able to hear and respond to another inspiring voice. He was attuned to the voice of the angel that allowed him not to follow the voice of cruelty as somehow the voice of God. With Abraham we move away from the representations and practices of a violent God to allow the birth in our human consciousness of a compassionate God. In the biblical stories we learn that the interface of human and divine is not a static one; it is an ecstatic, destabilizing relationship that changes our lives and generates something unprecedented.

In Jesus this divine, creative, connective impulse reaches a subversive radicalism. Born within a culture and a spiritual tradition, he passes the limits of kinship, descent, belonging, gender, and race to embrace every creature, even the opponent and death. Christ brings into the Universe a new consciousness of love, a new unity in creation. He undermines hierarchies, potentates, apparatuses of exclusion and inequality, our visible and invisible strategies to control and to dominate. With his subversive and inclusive love he strips us of the layered defenses of our personal and collective egos and makes us incarnated sons and daughters of the creative Impulse.

The spiritual Energy of the Universe, Abraham, Moses, Jesus, the Lovers of all spiritual traditions empower us today to offer our bodies as threads, nods, expansions of this love in places where the spirit is suffocated, excluded, or buried. How do we allow the Spirit of love to be poured into our hearts? What kind of connections do we advocate for in these dramatic and stormy times we are living in? If we do not create a world based on love, kindness, generosity, ethical and ecological sensitivity, social justice, and peace, then the world itself will not work, wars will perpetuate, and an environmental catastrophe will be our destiny.

Are we listening closely enough to the conflicts and contradictions of our time to interpret them as a kind and challenging warning from the Universe? Is he not telling us that the ethical, the spiritual, and the physical are intrinsically bound together in the commandment of love? Is he not soliciting us that when we build a society based on greed, selfishness, materialism, and endless consumption disaster will follow?

To conclude, I would like to linger over an image at the Civic Museum of Sansepolcro in Tuscany. It is a polyptych by Piero della Francesca. The central panel portrays a *Virgin of Mercy* (Gaia-Sophia-Spirit), a merciful Madonna who enfolds in her mantle all kinds of peoples kneeling around her in prayer. The Madonna has a sort of impersonal stare, as if she has transformed every selfish attachment into a receptive, welcoming, blossoming field of compassion. With all of creation we are wrapped in God's mercy, and we are empowered to be creative extensions of this mantle of Grace in all the situations of our life.

Year C

First Sunday of Advent

Jer 33:14-16; 1 Thess 3:12–4:2;
Luke 21:25-28, 34-36

The great mythologist Joseph Campbell said, "The Catholic religion is a *poetic religion*. Every month [and season] has its poetic and spiritual value."[1] We can be grateful that our spiritual life is flavored every year by different liturgical seasons that infuse rhythm and inspiration to our journey on Earth, transforming our bodies into thresholds of awareness and enlightenment. Intertwined with the rolling of time, these sacred seasons leaven the dough of our existences, opening us to the creative energy of the Spirit in our personal and collective experience. Above all they connect us to the ongoing manifestation of God, whose matrix is the invincible and revolutionary love of the paschal mystery.

Today we cross the doors of Advent that will culminate with Epiphany. Day after day we are initiated by the liturgy to the event of God's birth in our life. Dawning time between darkness and light, Advent awakens us to the transcendence of time, which is not meaningless repetition and closure but a still-emerging process, open to the future, full of God's promises, of unexpressed possibilities, of what has not yet happened.

Paul expresses this spirit of Advent in a powerful image of joyous hope and eager waiting. He addresses the believers in Rome, saying, "We know that the whole creation [groans aloud the pangs of new birth.] . . . We ourselves, who have the first fruits of the Spirit, groan inwardly. . . . If we hope for what we do not see, we wait for it with patience" (Rom 8:22-23, 25).

We are living in a restless and meandering process of birthing, together with the whole creation. We are groaning aloud within a genesis of the Cosmos that lasts for billions of years from the time of the big bang, full of novelty and dissolution, gain and loss, pain and renewal. This laboring Universe has collaborated to bring us here, to this moment, so that we can wake up and participate with the birthing of new things that are different from what already exists or has existed. Our sacred name for the Energy that forms and transforms every existing being is *God*, who has never ceased to become matter, web of life, consciousness, flowing into new forms when the right time comes.

In this Advent we celebrate the coming God as perennial newness of love. Love is ecstatic, constantly transcending itself toward greater depth, embodiment, and openness. In Jesus this divine Action becomes radical incarnation. He dissolves the distant, sacrificial, and almighty God. Crashing the cultural and religious walls of separation of his time, Jesus seizes with wonder the divine presence within the ordinariness and messiness of our world, committing himself to what can be changed, healed, included, enjoyed, and wildly hoped. He is the Messiah that breathes under the fragile tents of our hopes and yearnings, entering through the small door of every day, every moment, and every gesture.

Today's readings focus our attention to the coming of God not in an ideal situation, but rather in an environment of suffering and despair. Jeremiah is living when Jerusalem is under siege; the prophet himself is in prison; destruction and deportation are imminent.

Luke writes his account of events after the destruction of Jerusalem, and the core of his gospel speaks of Jesus' demise that becomes the womb of God's creativity. Hope, watchful waiting, and faithful responsibility are the responses of God's inspiration when worlds are collapsing. Something new is arising within, from unknown territories, disrupting the present system and its keepers: a breakthrough in consciousness.

Do we recognize the coming God under the cloud of vulnerability and breakdown in which we are living? The Middle East is struggling for democracy and freedom. Palestine has been recognized as a state by the United Nations. Other developing countries try to emerge, even among wars, voicing their rights and their wild hopes. Europe toils, in fear of a confederation of states. The United Nations conference for climate change in Qatar is pursuing, among contradictions, a new agreement to decrease greenhouse gases, despite their increasing in many countries. Communities of believers throughout the world are exploring new paths of faith where women, genders, and differences are welcomed and intertwined, in a shared celebration of love. The United States is going through an exciting and arduous multiethnic experience that is changing its blood, face, and soul.

God is coming.
Are we ready to start getting ready,
despite clouds, crises, and pains?
We are alert, still. We are patient, wait, and pray.
We prepare the unknown birth, the still unimagined visions,
knowing that there is more at stake than we can figure.
A blessing awaits us all in this laboring time.
May the grace and peace of the season, in which we enter, be ours.

Note

1. Joseph Campbell, *The Hero's Journey: Joseph Campbell on His Life and Work*, ed. Phil Cousineau (Novato, CA: New World Library, 2003), 6.

Holy Family

1 Sam 1:20-22, 24-28; 1 John 3:1-2, 21-24; Luke 2:41-52

As I was meditating this week on the meaning of the Holy Family, I was struck by this book title: *The Holy or the Broken: Leonard Cohen, Jeff Buckley, and the Unlikely Ascent of "Hallelujah." Hallelujah* is one of my favorite songs, and it is the most performed rock song in history. It was recorded as part of an album that was rejected by Cohen's longtime record label. Three years after his debut album, *Grace*, Jeff Buckley would be dead, his only album largely unknown, and *Hallelujah* still unreleased as a single. Yet this obscure song became an international anthem for human triumph and tragedy. I find this queer combination of the holy and of the broken in the song *Hallelujah* also appropriate for the Holy Family, for the event of incarnation, for our families and communities!

There is at the same time something holy, unconventional, and broken in this family incarnated by Joseph, Mary, and Jesus: a holy brokenness that connects us to the mystery of our lives. The Holy radiates as a new revelation of love that breaks the conventions and separations of a human congregation. The Holy shines in the appearance of an angel to Mary, precarious and elusive yet so trustworthy and fruitful—similar to the experience of listening to our own inspirations and visions. The Holy glimmers in the troubled heart of Joseph, who swings between his fear of Mary being exposed to public disgrace and his faith in the incomprehensible to whom to say yes. The Holy shimmers in this family capable of hosting the mystery of a fragile child who is in need of everything and yet outside any attempt of possession. There is a baby arriving in an uneasy situation. They are anxious, they don't understand, but they trust; they embrace

73

an unknown future that creates something that would not be possible within a reassuring security.

Jesus in today's gospel addresses his parents in the temple, saying, "Did you not know that I must be in my Father's house?" We discover that in Jesus the house of God becomes every human being who accepts the invitation to pass from self-centeredness to an embracing, enlarging of heart. The Letter of John introduces us into the revelation of the Holy: in Jesus "we are now God's children." Broken are the walls of separation with the other, with the world, and with God. Holy is now the whole human family and the Cosmos, since Jesus has become the consciousness we have of being generated by God. The selfless love of God has been poured out by the power of the Spirit. It is out of this love that we are and continue to be created. We become the vehicle of Energy that breaks the walls of separation. The Holy Child involves us with his birth not in an excluding sect but in a cosmic dance: shepherds and animals, angels and stars, dreams and wisdom of the nations, and, later, the multitude of people that become God's favorites: children and women, sinners and pagans, poor and sick.

Today, in spite of existing systems of domination, violence, selfishness, and consumerism, the Holy Family happens wherever we activate an alternative Energy based on generosity, love of the excluded, justice for the powerless, embrace of the rainbow of loving human relationship, care for all creatures and our planet Earth.

We live in dark times: many countries are still in the grip of violence and hostility, in the spiral of injustice, in the refusal of diminishing the carbon dioxide production, and in the coercion of gender discrimination. May these holy days attune us to a different sense of existence, a different future for the large, interdependent society we have become. And in the spirit of the holy/broken family I would like to express an inclusive prayer of Bernard Schlager[1] that may reflect the divine, all-embracing love.

> O God, Mother and Father of Us All, . . .
>
> Like your son, Jesus of Nazareth, who blessed a variety of human relationships rooted in love, may we have the wisdom and grace to foster, strengthen, and support all loving relationships and all families.

May your command to love one another as you have loved us, O God, cause us to pay heed to the movement of your Holy Spirit, who calls us in the here and now to embrace the rainbow of loving human relationships that reflect your love for all of humanity in its wonderful diversity.

May we speak out courageously when others try to pass laws that exclude, diminish, or demonize other persons and their families because of who they are and whom they love. May we take to heart what we know to be true: that where love and charity prevail, you are to be found.

We ask this, as always, through your Many Holy Names. Amen.

Note

1. Bernard Schlager, "How About a Prayer for All Marriages (And All Committed Relationships Rooted in Love)?," *The Huffington Post* (January 3, 2012), http://www.huffingtonpost.com/bernard-schlager-phd/how-about-a-prayer-for-al_b_1181145.html.

Year C

Third Sunday in Ordinary Time

Neh 8:2-4a, 5-6, 8-10; 1 Cor 12:12-30;
Luke 1:1-4; 4:14-21

In his inaugural and inspired discourse in Washington, at the mid-term of his mandate, President Obama asserted, "We have always understood that when times change, so must we; that fidelity to our founding principles requires new responses to new challenges." I found that this idea—fidelity to founding principles as only possible through the constant reinvention of them in the changing contexts of time—is what unites the assembly gathered around the president in Washington, around the scribe Ezra in the square of Jerusalem, and around Jesus in the synagogue of Nazareth.

I want to share with you some reflections about the liturgical assembly and the Spirit who is forging every "today" of our lives.

We pause, first, upon the *liturgical frame* in which we celebrate and give meaning to the events of our lives. We are not born rugged individualists, alone and self-sufficient, but we are always involved in a celebration of life that surpasses, connects, and exults our singularities in a chorus of different bodies. Isn't it interesting that from the very beginning—from the big bang of Genesis—God slowly gathers the assembly of life from light, stars, earth, to humankind, creating a cosmic liturgy of interconnected diversities? And the last book of the Bible, Revelation, envisions at the end of time another assembly of all creation, where the glory of God is the light, and mourning, crying, and pain will be no more.

People were gathered at the foot of Mount Sinai when Moses received a law meant to soften the violence of our relationships. And then Nazareth, where all were amazed at the gracious words that came from the mouth of Jesus. And then the assembly of Vatican II, our congregation at Incarnation Monastery, and the network liturgy of our multicultural world.

In the second reading Paul describes us as a body composed of many members, including our frictions and vulnerabilities, gifts, wounds, and hopes, all embraced and transformed by the radical, overflowing love of Jesus, giver of abundant life. We are various subjects and identities gathered together by God's love in our diversities, ethnicity, class, race, religion, sexuality, and gender, where everybody is worthy of recognition and expression. We are called to participate in liturgy as a field of compassion that challenges the powers that are at work to separate and to dominate in the world. We are called to participate in a liturgy of sons and daughters of God that embraces the whole earth, where we express awe and wonder at the grandeur and mystery of the Universe.

The second element I would like to voice is *the Spirit forging every today of our lives.* "*Today* is holy to the Lord your God"; "*Today* this Scripture has been fulfilled in your hearing"; "*Now* decisions are upon us." In the local assembly of Jerusalem, Nazareth, Washington, or Incarnation Monastery, there is a creative Word that resounds and connects us to a story from where we come: the Universe, the law, the multitude of the prophets, Jesus, the constitutions. Yet the faithfulness to these embodied words of life requires the responsibility and risk of new responses, interpretations, beginnings . . . even a subversion of them, when these words become oppressive or excluding structures or hierarchies. We cannot stay secured in the comfort zone of our knowledge or behavior. We cannot possess and fix the Spirit, but we are exposed to the changing, surprising, and unexpected tides of time that ask from us unprecedented answers: "For now decisions are upon us and we cannot afford delay."[1]

How can we kindle the embers from the ash of custom and uniformity, how to reinvigorate the fires of love? Can our worship communities embrace the new "intruders" that may or may not correspond to the modes of life in play within the present time? Do our political, economic, ethical, religious frames allow the emergence of these new subjects, bearers of Spirit? Immigrants and women, gender disparity and oppression, the multitude of colors, languages, and spiritual journeys as infinite ways through which the infinite God radiates, caring for each other and the Earth.

Today the Spirit rises as tongues of fire upon us and among us,
making of us a dance of diversity.
Today God is present in the embers of our words, silences, wounds,
bread, wine, bodies—in a cosmic, human, divine dance.
Today pain, grievance, weapons, and offenses burn
in the flame of Christ's love,
showing the depth of God's happiness buried in our heart.

Note

1. President Barack Obama, Second Inaugural Address (Washington, DC: January 21, 2013).

Third Sunday of Lent

Exod 3:1-8a, 13-15; 1 Cor 10:1-6, 10-12; Luke 13:1-9

The first time I leaned over the Grand Canyon, it was like plunging into the sheer immensity of time, laid out for my wonder and giddiness. After the first upheaval of the senses in front of this unfathomable depth, my gaze began to run through the multilayered rock face, each stratum a manifestation of the vast, adventurous, and creative story of our planet Earth. Each epoch engraved as petrified footprint on the canyon: the multifaceted adventure of life displayed in front of me! Pushing forward the glance of my imagination, I could go back to the roots of this immense journey, to our ancestors the stars, from where everything comes forth or, jumping ahead, I could figure the branches of this tree in the contemporary cyberspace, that immaterial mesh of flowing information and tech-devices that surround, contaminate, connect, and expand us. I felt the Grand Canyon was also an image of the various canyons of our cultures and religions, and of the small canyon that each of us carries inwardly, the many strata of ages, changes, and relationships that have molded and nurtured our existence.

I like to interpret the fig tree, mentioned in today's gospel, that a gardener takes care of and puts manure on as the vast tree of life with all its branches as it is embodied in the Grand Canyon. Throughout the awesome exodus of creation the divine and boundless Presence has continued to take care of the growing of cosmological, biological, and spiritual life, digging, nurturing, raising, pulling forward, renewing the journey of the Universe and of our personal and social life. As the second reading points out, it is a hard and challenging journey passing through the sea, the cloud, and the desert; a process marked by trials and errors, meanderings, accelerations and breakdowns, covenants, growth and extinction, blossoming, collapse, and ecological pressures that cause the unfurling of life. Indeed, the same failures, barrenness, adversity, and pains, like decomposing manure, have created the possibility of newness, the breakthrough of evolutionary leaps: some of the greatest catastrophes in our planet's life history have spawned the greatest creativity.

At different moments of our open-ended story, the impulse of divine action is at stake, taking care of creation that it may continue and blossom. The creator Spirit needs somebody willing to challenge stasis, conventions, or status quo; to continue the journey of self-discovery; someone who can draw hope from loss and beauty from ugliness.

Generation after generation the blowing Spirit needs someone to reimagine the world, someone who hears the cry of the distressed, who transcends the wall of the already known, who crosses the Red Sea of captivity toward further spaces of freedom. Someone who speaks words that make others dream and envision, gestures of scandalous love, music, pictures, or technologies that speed up justice and equality for all people; someone who takes responsibility for all the creatures and for planet Earth.

I am the God of Abraham, Moses and Sarah, Buddha, Mary, and Einstein, John XXIII and Martin Luther King Jr.; I am the God of each one of you, who agrees to be manure for the world, who responds to the incessant and divine movement of transcendence at the core of the human heart. I Am. I am the blossoming of the past, the inexhaustible potentiality of the now, and I will be the ever-newness of your future, more vast than the present moment can hold. I am the burning bush of the cross, the divine who becomes humble and vulnerable—until death. I am the power of Love that is able to raise life even from the process of the decomposition of a body. I am the one who rolls away the stone of violent inherited instincts from hearts and baptizes you in the infinite life of Christ.

Do we believe that we are manure for the garden of God? Do we believe that our shadow and messiness and the ugliness of the world are the field of transformation of divine action?

We are your manure, Gardener of life.
We are also the Gardeners of our ravaged fellows, and of our planet.
Sometimes we are also a barren fig tree,
a community that is not hearing the cry of the world
and has condemned herself to demise.
God of many names, manifestations, and ages,
we invoke your Spirit of resurrection, rejuvenation, and compassion.

Year C

Fifth Sunday of Lent

Isa 43:16-21; Phil 3:8-14; John 8:1-11

The American playwright Tennessee Williams wrote, "When you look at a piece of delicately spun glass you think of two things: *how beautiful it is and how easily it can be broken.*"[1] This realization sounds for me as the hallmark of our existence, the acknowledgment of the inevitable entwining of beauty, and the potential for being broken.

There are times in our life where we experience the anxiety about the fragility of our experience that can fall to pieces. These are narrow and obscure passages, crucibles of crises that unexpectedly supervene, moments that force us to distinguish between the essential and the marginal, to discriminate our priorities, maybe to discover a precious pearl in the mess of our life. The apostle Paul would say that these moments compel us to distill the good—maybe the supreme good—from the rubbish (Phil 3:8).

Our Lenten journey is constellated by these storm cones that prepare us to face the supreme crises, the brutal assassination of the Compassionate, the Just, and the Healer. We are reminded of these passages: the temptations in the desert, the transfiguration, the Samaritan woman at the well, and the prodigal son. Today's gospel is also the dramatic rising of beauty and love from the vulnerability of our human experience, exposed to violence, and the unexpected gift of a new beginning, of an unprecedented liberation!

We are informed, from the evangelist, that we are orbiting in the gravitational area of the temple, of the law, of the religion: a very dangerous area, a minefield! Why is it so? Because there is no major force that bursts out more than our identification with the powers we consider divine or transcendent, that assure us with their protection and prescribed order.

We can in fact brandish the name of our God to obtain a favorable result, the victory of our cause against the cause of the other, our true god overcoming the false, weak, corrupted god of the other. A seized god to impose a sacred or cultural order, and to eradicate all the ones that with their very difference or behavior challenge our desires of control and security, standardization and colonization.

The religious, but also the social and political establishment, can reinforce the human and very dangerous *idea of purity*, one of the most problematic issues of our human history: the war as purifier, the Christian hell. The idea of purity is connected with the idea to extract from the world a pure form, preserved from disorder, contamination, and hybridization. It reflects the desire to clearly separate the sacred from the profane, the right from the wrong, the normal from the abnormal, and what we considered natural from what we label as unnatural. The quest for purity tends to simplify, to clean, to remove, to exclude, to homologate, to condemn, and to sacrifice. The different becomes the enemy or the heretic, the sinner, the deviant or sick, the insane or wild to be controlled, facing the possibility of being struck down.

Our society and our churches ooze in these kinds of phobia: against the alien (*xenophobia*); against women, so that a church can decide to investigate feminine religious communities (*misogynia*); against every attempt to mix or connect different aspects of our experience, religions, or cultures (*mixophobia*); against same-sex relationships (*homophobia*). Sooner or later the destructive scapegoat mechanism triggers off, and there will be victims on the battlefield!

This scapegoat dynamism is at the core of today's gospel. Jesus takes the risk to get in touch with the accused woman (but where is the man with whom she was caught in adultery?). He turns things upside-down and reveals an unpredictable, new face of God: the God of love and compassion that exceeds the law, the merits, and the virtues. Through these empathizing experiences Jesus himself will become the target of violence: a huge, definitive stone will be placed upon his corpse and his story. And yet, the revolutionary energy of God's love, the forever eluding encapsulation in orderly schemata, the dissolver of rigid design, the disturbing and fresh Wellspring will appear as an overflowing, unimaginable source of novelty!

How beautiful it is, and how easily it can be broken.

It is not easy, in fact, to take a distance from what we are used to considering the truth, to distance ourselves from the identification with our personal or our collective ego! How may we lose the weight, the force of gravity of punitive thoughts, of offensive actions and retaliations? How do we distance from the painful inheritances of our cultures or religions, from their terror, abuse, and humiliation, when they become sources of exclusiveness, marginalization, and offense? How can we convert them into something that allows growth and forgiveness, possibility of change and *resurrection*?

Facing this wave of violence and intolerance, what does Jesus do? He bends down. He creates a space of silence, a detachment that interrupts the outcry of the crowd. He exposes himself to the energies of the unknown, of the unthought. Maybe our spaces of prayer, meditation, mindfulness, and silence create in our life this holy space where the established values, what we were taught about religion and God crumble away. And the stones slowly become sand, and in the sand we are able to write new words of life, to mold a new creation, a re-creation of the world. We write words no more on the stone tables, but in the living flesh of our hearts, guided by the Spirit of creative and prophetic love. "I am about to do a new thing; / now it springs forth, do you not perceive it?" (Isa 43:19).

The good news of the gospel invites us today to bend our gaze to ourselves or, to say it differently, to convert our attention *from the outside toward the within*, to stop the game of not being responsible for *our* vulnerability, shadows, shortcomings, and mistakes. I feel that if there is not such an illumination, we will always accuse the other, searching for the guilty upon which to pronounce our verdict.

By accepting and taking responsibility for our vulnerability, we can discover a righteousness that doesn't come from ourselves, but comes from trusting in Love (Phil 3:9), a benevolence that empowers us to welcome the limits and the riches of the other. Jesus inaugurates a space of gratuitousness. The stones fall away. The woman is lifted up. And all the bystanders continue their journey lightened, relieved, and eased.

What do we do with our faith? Will we still use Jesus' name as a religious weapon of exclusiveness and dominion, or as a crucible where we are permanently disarmed, are graced, and take responsibility for one another?

How beautiful it is, and how easily it can be broken.

Note

1. Tennessee Williams, *The Glass Menagerie* (New York: New Directions, 2011), 55.

Easter Vigil

Rom 6:3-11; Luke 24:1-12

A seismic question originates from the earthquake of the dark-luminous night of Easter, a question that crosses space and time to resound among us tonight: *Why do you look for the Living among the dead?* With the women going to the tomb at early dawn, with all creatures and human seekers of the story, of the Universe, we also participate in the night of suffering, corpses, brokenness, failures, failings, fallings. At the heart of these open wounds of sorrow, vulnerability, and dominion, the paschal question opens our senses to another, unexpected shore of happiness, the promise of life ahead, the taste of fullness.

This night, God, you question death, the powers of death. The question that you arise in this night is Jesus, the Living one, the destruction and glorification of his body—of all bodies—by your love, stronger than any human production of violence and death.

As we well know, powers and world systems that mold cultures and behaviors hardly like their orders to be questioned and challenged. Economics, politics, religion, and knowledge more than often like submission, obedience, and control. They like to give answers and imperatives, not raise a query, or to queer. As the dangerous memory of Easter continues to radiate in human hearts and creation, Jesus' revolutionary Spirit doesn't stop shaking the destructive powers of death and pain as he did along the roads of Galilee, acting as a rule breaker—empowered by God's unconditional love. As if Jesus were looking for openings, where we had been walled up.

In the tombs of the world, an upsetting question arises tonight that violates the established boundaries of this world, the status quo rooted in our fears: *Why do you look for the Living among the dead?*

And the Spirit within us says, You can be damned sure that this question is not going to stop. In our time we are experiencing both a very great death and a very great birth. How do we incarnate this destabilizing question, moving between cross and resurrection?

Every time we break the tomb of the world as it is, with its injustice, you arise, Jesus. When we welcome women to crack our hierarchical and patriarchal culture, you arise, God. When we ban guns that are expansions and explosions of our violent hearts, you arise, Christ. When we allow marriage equality to committed lovers, beyond gender and discrimination, you arise, Spirit.

When we are able to embrace and to bend over the shadow, the repressed, the denied in our bodies, in our relationship with others, you arise, Jesus. When we honor creation without greed and exploitation, growing in respect, awe, and gratitude for our planet Earth, you arise, God.

When we experience God in the tenuous and perilous territory of our life as a presence that suggests, intimates, or whispers, rather than commands and determines, you arise, Christ. When we get closer to the burning bush of God stripped from reasons, claims, or pretentions, in a silent and ardent prayer, you arise, Spirit.

Year C

Third Sunday of Easter

Acts 5:27-32, 40b-41; Rev 5:11-14; John 21:1-14

Children, have you no food? "No," they answered (see John 21:5).

People usually stumble over a stone, a step, or a jut. This week I stumbled over the power of this "no" expressed by the disciples.

Let us now pause together with this hopeless and unfruitful *no* that contains all the "nos" we meet in the sailing of our life. We may feel inclined to read the paschal mystery in a linear fashion where life is simply victorious over death. Yet in this way, we risk glossing over a more mixed experience of death *and* life. This scene by the Sea of Tiberias reminds us instead that the boat of our life can at any moment run into uncertain and discomforted waters of despair and defeat, impossibility, depression, or stasis. And that every time we can feel embraced when we experience a hearty space willing to welcome our impasses, asking—as did Jesus—what the cause is of our suffering.

Children, have you no food?

Today I feel that each one of us is invited by the risen Christ—the one who has himself crossed the sea of death—to acknowledge with empathy our personal and communal brokenness and deficiency, to embrace the "nos" of our personal, social, and international seas, where we don't catch anything. Many are indeed the seas of Tiberias:

We look powerlessly and with sadness at the flowing of oil along the roads of Mayflower, Arkansas; at the tensions with North Korea, with a nuclear threat again in the air; at the slaughters in Syria and Africa; or at the suicide bombings in Afghanistan, Pakistan, and Iraq. We look powerlessly and with sadness at the assault weapons being used in massacres in the United States; at the denigration of women in the world; at the current economic, gender, and ethnic discriminations. In all these waters we don't make a catch. Yet, it is at these critical moments of our personal and community life, where stasis *and* transformation is at stake, after a struggle or a defeat at daybreak, that we can be surprised by a subtle presence there, that we may call God or we are awakened by an unexpected, urgent voice:

Throw the net over the right side of the boat.

In a lack of meaning that plagues us we may be ready to begin again, to move from our unfruitful space, and to connect with self-giving Love, the fundamental energy of the Universe, the source of overabundant life and beauty. The Sea of Tiberias teaches us that the feast of life, the embodiment of who we are, the sharing of our gifts is not something that just happens, nor does it all happen in a straight line or all at one time. As Joan Chittister says, "The song we are meant to sing does not come to us whole. It grows in us . . . over the years," and we go through risky passages.[1]

I feel that one of the great risky passages where we are called as humanity to cast our net today is an amazing *new understanding and awareness* that we are a large, interweaving body of life in formation that overcomes the small and separate logics of our personal, political, economic, or religious interests. We can be blinded by our culture and ego to the spiritual dimension of social life: by focusing wholly on humans' desire for things, we fail to perceive the power of humans' desire for love, community, solidarity, and connection with others; of our common humanity as authentic presence of the Spirit; of our deep dialogue with creation, earth, and Cosmos, from which we emerge.

A new era of life, a new face of Christ is rising from within our human, secular, daily shore, inviting us to a banquet of sharing where riches are multiplied by the divine energy of Love. Indeed, it is toward a wholeness of love that the divine Energy is attracting us through the creative waters of her grace.

Goddess-God of many Names, Faces, and Gifts
the creativity of the Universe is not evenly distributed;
there are places where its intensity reaches a high,

like the burning bush of Jesus,
epiphany of your compassion for the world
stronger than violence and death.

Awaken us to this new galaxy of consciousness in formation,
to these inner circles and currents of incarnation,
of infinite fecundity of your love.

That we can learn to share vulnerability and joy,
loss and gift, collapse and hope,
wisdom and unknown,
death and life.
Alleluia!

Note

1. Joan Chittister, *Following the Path: The Search for a Life of Passion, Purpose, and Joy* (New York: Random House, 2012), 44.

Ascension of the Lord

Acts 1:1-11; Eph 1:17-23; Luke 24:46-53

Today our multifaceted Easter journey is nourished by another enlightening event: the ascension of Jesus taken up into heaven, into the heart of God. We are so accustomed by science fiction literature and media to see flying heroes and superheroes—*Star Trek*, *The Avengers*, *The Matrix*—that it is not difficult for us to imagine Jesus defying gravity, ascending like a rocket into the sky, reuniting with the same Source that sent him into the world.

Why are we so deeply attracted to sky, to openness, to eternity? Is God a *break* in the clouds of our life bounded by time, restlessly defying the gravity of our narrow-minded selves? What are these seeds of ascension, of limitlessness sown in our bodies, and expressed in so many works and dreams of imagination: myths, sacred and profane stories, spiritual journeys, artifacts, and scientific explorations? And are not our technologies ways to expand our human possibilities beyond the given limitations, in a process of ascension toward a better quality and web of life? A mysterious *instinct* for eternity pulses in our bodies and pulls us out from imposed limits toward new possibilities, further meanings, and greater fullness of life.

There are moments in our lives when we are driven out of ourselves and taken up to a greater sky or a deeper mystery: when love shines and our hearts catch fire; in unpredictable moments of discovery and illumination; in instants of intimacy with another person, where we feel uplifted and broadened out; when suffering breaks the container of our armored existence, and we are softened, opened to greater compassion.

From another perspective, Pierre Teilhard de Chardin considered evolution as a *biological ascent* toward more complex life forms: from

molecules, to single cells, to self-conscious human beings, still moving toward a greater aliveness and connectedness. We are part of an
immense and risky process of death and resurrection, taken up by
an attractive force that works within and lies ahead: the inexhaustible
creativity and relational nature that we call God. The superabundant
grace of God's mystery is an ever-widening ripple of participation
until it reaches all space, time, and particles of matter and of consciousness.

In the ascension of Jesus we can foreshadow, as a yeast and a
prophecy, this attraction of all creation into the fullness and ecstatic
dance of God's love. With Jesus we are carried up into heaven, which
is nothing less than the heart of God's love, stronger than all constraining patterns that reproduce fear, violence, and death. Today we
get closer to the *paradox* of ascension, which is at the same time a
descent: descent of God into creation, in the humanity of Jesus, embracing suffering, failure, injustice, and death; descent that expands
life to new dimensions, to deeper intimacy, freedom, and responsibility. It happens that in our spiritual life we often ascend when we
bend over.

One day, Archbishop Oscar Romero realized his friend and fellow-
priest Rutilio had been brutally murdered while fighting for the poor.
From that moment, captured by God's compassionate affection,
Romero was urged to *descend*, to break the frontiers of his religious
status, and to embrace the vulnerable condition of the needy. He
began his ascension to God, attracted by justice, inclusion, and
liberation on Earth.

We descend with you, God,
when we recognize forces of resistance in us and among us:
brutal violence, economic divide, women's marginalization,
conquering knowledge, depletion of our Earth, religious power,
ethnic and gender exclusions.

We ascend to you, God,
when we embrace the amazing cosmic process that allowed
Jesus to emerge,
and we consent to be opened by your unpredictable future,
by your alluring love.

We are lifted up to your heart, God,
when we welcome each other in our diversities,
as a celebration of your overjoyed communion.

We are taken up in your light, God,
when we surrender to your silent presence,
and believe that also our darkness and wounds
are particles of your bright abyss.

Year C

Body and Blood of Christ
Gen 14:18-20; 1 Cor 11:23-26; Luke 9:11b-17

I begin with a quote of Pope Francis, who declared some time ago, "If investments in the banks fail, 'Oh, it's a tragedy,' . . . but if people die of hunger or don't have food or health, nothing happens. This is our crisis today."[1]

A sense of crisis pervades our world today, not different from the deserted place where the disciples of Jesus were, in a day drawing to a close, and with a huge crowd hungry and thirsty: hungry for jobs, health, civil rights, human dignity, meaningful life, and peace. Not only the body of humanity but the entire body of the Earth faces dire threats because of climate disruption, pollution, and population growth. When the body of Jesus was broken in Jerusalem by the powers of violence and injustice, he opened new territories of freedom and love.

Today, old behaviors and patterns are also breaking down, and reality itself is being transformed in unexpected ways. A new body of Christ is emerging, including all creation. We could feel powerless and overwhelmed like the friends around Jesus: "We have no more than five loaves and two fish, but what is this in comparison with the crowd, with the huge problems we are facing?" Maybe we can find comfort and direction pausing on the three gestures expressed by Jesus in the gospel: care, blessing, and sharing.

Care. Jesus invites his friends to have people sit down, establishing a welcoming relationship. Jesus does not send them away in resignation or discomfort; he enacts a liturgy of hospitality. As sons and daughters of God's grace, ministers of God's compassion, this gesture elicits a receptive mind and an open heart: Do we really care about these persons? Are we open to release any unease in ourselves in order to welcome these persons no matter their status, gender, story, or brokenness? The spirit of Jesus enhances our imaginative powers and our capacity to be loving and kind, generous and caring for others, ethically and ecologically sensitive in our behavior, and able to experience others as embodiments of the divine nature.

Blessing. Jesus invites us to be open not only to the others but to the source of every "otherness," to the unfathomable Fountain of self-giving love that we call God. With gratefulness and radical amazement we are receivers and processors of the creative energy that from the beginning is forging the body of the Universe, pours the blood of life, consciousness, beauty in the unfolding cosmic adventure. Our blessing today corresponds to our entry in an era of universal consciousness. We are awakened to a mystery greater than us, increasingly able to transcend the tendency to look at the physical world merely in separate, utilitarian, or mechanistic terms. We discover that all expressions of life are connected, interdependent, particles of a divine body, a corporate body of Christ, a big body of love.

Sharing. Jesus first shares his love with us. He loves us to the end: This is my body that is for you. Jesus breathes out and radiates his Spirit of resurrection, the radical love shared with the Source and the Spirit, a love stronger than death. Jesus invites us to live our divine nature in our bodies, our relationships, our careers, and our communities.

The Eucharist table is an ecosystem of sharing. Where there is unfair possession we are invited to create circulation of life-giving bread and love, freedom and learning, responsibility and joy. Where there is excluding competition we are invited to enliven forms of cooperation and mutual enhancement. Where there is dominion that dehumanizes we are invited to use power in the right sense through service.

May we be always hungry and thirsty for Love.
May our hearts and minds be soft and receptive to God's abundant life.
May our bodies have open doors and windows
to welcome the approaching, unknown future.

May we welcome, bless, and share this Universe,
this Earth, this time,
as a lavish banquet of grace God is setting.

Note

1. Rachel Donadio, "Francis' Humility and Emphasis on the Poor Strike a New Tone at the Vatican," *The New York Times* (May 25, 2013), http://www.nytimes.com/2013/05/26/world/europe/pope-francis-changes-tone-at-the-vatican.html?_r=0.

Nativity of John the Baptist (Vigil Mass)

Jer 1:4-10; 1 Pet 1:8-12; Luke 1:5-17

Among the many secrets that the Universe has recently revealed to us there is a particular one that I would like to point out, as it may light up today's celebration of the birth of John the Baptist.

We have discovered that the fabric of the entire cosmic process has been shaped and continues to evolve with the help of two opposing and creative tensions: *a movement of attraction* that pushes things together and *a movement of expansion* that presses life ever further into creative, exploratory intensities. If we pause and pay attention, we realize with amazement that the enormity of creativity that surrounds us is profoundly *exploratory*. In everything that exists there is an impulse that transcends the limitations of things as they are and gives rise to something new: from the big bang to stars, galaxies, and planets; from the Earth to oceans, animals, and consciousness; from our ancestors to the vast unfolding tapestry of cultural development that brings us to this present moment, to the mysterious aspirations that murmur in our bodies.

We can name *Spirit* this ecstatic pressure bubbling within the heart of matter and time that tries to open new paths of life, new organs of love and inclusion, justice and freedom, connection and respect for all beings. And is not the event of John the Baptist an *ecstatic urgency* and call to a personal, spiritual, and social change through which God prepares a new revelation, a new leap in seeing and relating with each other? The people wonder about the future of this newborn child shrouded in mystery that escapes from their grasp: "What then will this child *become*?" (Luke 1:66).

Who is this elusive child that we celebrate? It is doubtless the Baptist, but it is also our personal child as an expression of the depths of ourselves; it is the life of the communities we are generating; it is the birth of our world in a vast, troubled, and changing conscious-ness, where the paths are uncertain and winding, and we wonder: "What then will this child become?" Neighbors and relatives around this child are going to call him with the name of his father but Elizabeth interrupts the reassuring repetition of the same. With the energy and the inspiration that bursts forth from her heart she says, "Hell no. He is to be called John," which means *God-shows-mercy.* As Elizabeth did, will we also be able to spell *in a new way* what is emerging as a grace of God in our life or history? Or are we trying to frame the divine newness in the wineskins of old patterns and behaviors, hushing up the process of freedom and consciousness that the Spirit is spilling over into our hearts and cultures? Will we be able to show God's mercy in the midst of a transition that is prom-ising but also exposed to destructiveness and exclusion?

"By the tender [compassion] of our God, / the dawn from on high will break upon us" (Luke 1:78). A crack happens in the crust of the standard and dominant religiosity. Pangs of labor begin. Contractions and tensions spread to the whole area. At the margins of the empire, the Baptist sows the barren field with new seeds of compassion. He prepares the hearts to welcome the greater love of Christ who in-novates our hearts of stone with tender, new hearts of flesh. John's eventual martyrdom forces one of his disciples to make a life-changing decision: Does he continue the exploratory, prophetic journey of his mentor or does he return to his native village to continue the work as a carpenter? Jesus chooses to go on. He pushes forward the edge from where John left off, changing water into fire, and law into grace. Breaking down all the walls of separation, opposition, and exclusion until he transforms the last, mortal wall of evil into a new passage of goodness and life.

Are not all of us sort of Baptists, forerunners of the ever-coming and innovating Christ? Is not each one of us an embodiment of God's perennial birth? A lot of exploratory intensities are at play today. Peoples promoting the cross-fertilization of religions and spirituali-ties; the Nuns on the Bus tour, opening ways of justice and inclusion; different worldviews and practices are emerging to save our planet from collapsing; immigration issues open up ethical and spiritual questions about excluding boundaries, and property.

We conclude with a prayer composed by Rev. Kendyll Gibbons:[1]

There comes a time to break the silence.
There comes a time to move beyond the fear.
There comes a time to speak one's truth, even if it will not be
    welcome.
There comes a time to call into question what has gone before;
To resist the weight of the past.
There comes a time for the singing of a new song.
For a different way of being,
There comes a time when the truth shall at last make us free.

. . . .

Holding us so gently in their love
That all at once the impossible is possible,
And we cross over to the other side of whatever bondage held us.
There comes a time when the truth at last makes us free,
And in that moment is the salvation of the world.

Note

1. Kendyll Gibbons, "Prelude," The Integrity of Pride, http://uupuertorico
.org/Sermons/pride.htm.

Twelfth Sunday in Ordinary Time
Zech 12:10-11; 13:1; Gal 3:26-29; Luke 9:18-24

I invite you to dive into two expressions we heard in the gospel and in the letter of Paul to the Galatians: "[You are] the Messiah of God" (Luke 9:20) and "All of you are one in Christ Jesus" (Gal 3:28). What do the people experience, what are the vibrations they feel getting in contact with Jesus, considering him the Messiah?

Who is Messiah? Maybe the one with healing energy and sacred vision who enhances each life it touches, honoring our vulnerable and breakable body as a wellspring of divine glory. Or it may be a liberating force that frees us from social, economic, or religious constraints, awakening us to the essence of who we are. Or it is a life-giving relationship, instead of an exploitative, life-depleting one. Maybe Messiah is the experience of a person who, enflamed by the exuberance of life, breaks through the borders of the world petrified by the ruling powers, and unleashes the drive of love, imagination, justice, and the interchange with the sensuous earth.

Jesus walked beyond the boundaries of his religion and culture, traveling new paths of meaning, empowering us with a new vision of sons and daughters of the divine Mystery, even if this emergence alarmed the security services, the guardians of impassable borders of his time, who tried to destroy him. And yet, from his open wounds, Jesus released into creation a spirit of radical passion that still vibrates through the centuries, still gathers us around a table, still attracts and pulls forward so many hearts, bodies, ideals, and actions into a borderless kingdom of love!

There was known to be a piece of writing on a wall in an African village: "When at last I will appear at the presence of God, God will tell me: 'Show me your wounds,' and if I have no wounds, God will ask, 'Was there nothing worth fighting for?'" There has been and still exists in religions a distorted mystique of suffering, obedience, and inflexible zeal, as if suffering and sacrifice in themselves were the gateway to the ultimate Mystery. But for Jesus, it is the pain of others, the constraints of the world that become a catalyst for struggle. Messianic is the passionate desire of Jesus, and of all the spiritual men and women of history, to radiate abundance of life, what makes life better, fresh, alive, a relentless quest for justice, participation, inclusiveness, peace, and happiness.

This passion for a new creation, this feeling for the creative Mystery changes the tone of Jesus' injunction to take up our cross daily and to follow him. To take up our cross could mean that we are not seeking certainty and religious security, but rather the radical insecurity and risk that is the nature of the human journey and of the Christian path. We take up our gifts of innovation, envisioning, mindfulness, personal and communal responsibility, and we participate in the divine, disruptive new creation. "I will pour out a Spirit of compassion," says the prophet Zechariah. This spirit of compassion makes all of us "one in Christ Jesus" (Gal 3:28). "If anyone is in Christ," says Paul, "there is a new creation: everything old has passed away; see, everything has become new!" (2 Cor 5:17).

We are at a critical stage of a new spiritual awakening. Old patterns of cultural, social, political, or religious life give way to new ones. We are entering into a planetary consciousness of being one body-in-diversities, one large and sacred story with the Earth, the Universe, the microbic community, all sentient beings, and the technologies that surround and penetrate us. In this hyper-connected world we need a messianic revolution into a vision of our planet that avoids collapse and self-destruction and celebrates it as an unfolding, planetary civilization.

Are we learning to breathe as a living organism that communicates and supports differences and connections? Are we entering into the consciousness of the sons and daughters of the Eternal Breath who animates fish and bird, plant and technologies, wisdoms and cultures, past and unknown future?

Vivifying Spirit,
wellspring of lavish inspiration

and stunning beauty
throughout the journey of the Universe,
in the unexpected resurrection of Jesus:
be the catalyst in each one of us
to become one body in a manifold solidarity,
a new creation,
a space of reciprocity and wonder,
and of humility in front of the immensity of life.

Sixteenth Sunday in Ordinary Time

Gen 18:1-10a; Col 1:24-28; Luke 10:38-42

This Sunday we first rejoice that the heart of the divine Mystery is revealed *through* a banquet, a feast of shared friendship, forgiveness, and passionate love. Probably because our daily experience of life is exposed at every moment to threats of violence, aggression, and outrage, every culture has attributed a divine quality to hospitality. Coupled with relationships of power, survival, and competition, there is in us a generative force that makes room for another creature to blossom, to relate, and to love; a divine quality that shone with a generous intensity in Jesus.

The pulsing heart of our Christian faith is a gratuitous banquet to which all are invited with no boundaries or exclusions, despite our fear, suspicion, and revenge, till the capacity to embrace even the enemy and his deadly violence. Since the beginning, God made a place for everything that exists, grows, and expands. God emptied Godself in Jesus, to embrace everyone (Phil 2:7). The eternal Source loses itself for love. A table is set for us, guests of God's love, "For I have set you an example, that you also should do as I have done to you" (John 13:15).

Hospitality is gift, but also labor and an endless journey. The home of Martha and Mary reminds us that our relationships begin with a sharing of food and feelings, of what nourishes and unites us, and grow toward a further hospitality, *a listening heart*. A listening heart is God's heart pulsing in us, the presence of *Christ in us* (Col 1:27), the Divine flame turning our often ego-centered heart and mind toward the expansion of love. A listening heart makes compassionate room to welcome gifts and wounds, needs and joys, thirsts and hungers of each person, though there are many inhospitable places on Earth, and close to us: slices of humanity trampled, weeping, bleeding, and excluded.

In the highly insightful movie *Fruitvale Station*—from the name of the BART station in Oakland, where the final dramatic scene takes place—I was struck by the awful din in which people of color and police are dazed, the negation of listening and of hospitality. And in the middle of this howling atmosphere soaked with commotion, suspicion, and aggression, the fatal shot is fired.

A listening heart is grateful for the widening circles of hospitality, from ourselves to the Universe. The primal house that welcomes us is our planet Earth, with its bounty of flowing waters, air, skies, plants, and animals that have enabled our emergence, nourish and support us, but which we are thoughtlessly destroying. A listening heart hosts the *unknown*. God comes from the unknown, and as Unknown leads us to a discovery of dimensions we hadn't noticed or ever experienced before. How many times, consenting to a destabilizing event, we have been widened, discovered an unsuspected face of God and of ourselves!

These visitations are often subversive. Welcoming the alien guests, Abraham discovers in his life an unexpected fecundity of the divine Wanderer: next year Sarah will have a son. It was a hard labor to welcome the resurrected Christ on the way to Emmaus. It was a joyous surprise for the first Judeo-Christian community to discover that God worked with irony and improvisation *through* people who knew nothing of the Torah. It took a tremendous act of hospitality and courage for Peter, Paul, and the first followers of Jesus to welcome Gentiles who knocked down cultural and religious identities. Informed by the Spirit of love, early Christianity was able to host a significant amount of theological, liturgical, and human diversity in their midst, including women as protagonists of communities.

Who is the stirring Spirit we are challenged to host with listening hearts in our communities, churches, countries, and world today, beyond ethnic, gender, religious, economic, and environmental inhospitalities that respond to life with fear, coercion, and restoration of the past instead of hope and creativity?

Today's worldly liturgy hosts us not with a Tea Party agenda,
but with a menu of fascinating dishes and beverages:
a prayerful heart, a generative spirit, a creative openness,
a surprised wonder,
a sense of hope-filled and sacred activism,
the interconnectedness of all things,
the experience of the Divine here and now,
the welcoming of diversities,
and an orientation toward the future of a new creation.
That we can be embodiment of divine, unconditional hospitality!

Year C

Twentieth Sunday in Ordinary Time

Jer 38:4-6, 8-10; Heb 12:1-4; Luke 12:49-53

I came to bring fire to the Earth.

It sounds as though we are celebrating an incendiary Sunday!

In 2006 an alarming and disquieting documentary appeared: *An Inconvenient Truth.* In contrast to mainstream conviction that we were doing marvelously well in making a better and more prosperous world, the ecological survey dismantled this false assumption, showing with overwhelming evidence that it is the opposite case: global warming is revealed as human-made, and our future will be cataclysmic for all the Earth if we do not act immediately.

Hearing and seeing the devastating and hopeless consequences of our failure to act, we are awakened to a new, vital possibility: we can change the course of events with a deep transformation of our personal, communal, and economic behaviors, for the future of the Earth and of all living beings. Immediately, the choir of fossil fuel and tar sands companies denied the facts with threatening voices, similar to the ones at the time of the prophet Jeremiah: "This man is discouraging people by speaking such words to them. This man is seeking the harm of this people," or the words addressed to Jesus: "This man is a danger for the nation, he has a demon, he blasphemes."

At the beginning of his social and religious activism Jeremiah tried to initiate a change in the system, but after a while he reached the conclusion that the only way to achieve reform was for the present institutions to be abandoned and new ones created.

The paradoxical, scandalous aspect of the story of Jeremiah and many others today is that officials in charge identify the will of the

king, of the priests, or of the party line with the will of God, like what
happened at the time of Jesus, who embodied the fiery, compassionate face of his Abba but was demonized and killed like an outlaw.

We become so accustomed to our habitual way of seeing and acting
that we don't want to see what is really happening, that our world
is changing. And we humans often use the name of God to justify
our inertia, to stay in our comfort zone, or control zone, reluctant to
transform visions and values.

I came to bring fire to the Earth.

What is there, at the heart of the Universe, at the heart of women
and men of every age and culture who have been able to generate
new beginnings, to change the course of evolution and of humanity,
opening new paths to life, beyond boundaries and conventions?
There is a sacred flame that burns at the heart of these people, at the
heart of each one of us: a longing for justice, a passion for freedom,
a care for the outcast and the sufferer, the yearning for an expanded
community of love on Earth. It is the burning bush of God's dangerous love, a transformative and surprising force that upsets any
achieved and oppressing equilibrium kneaded with fears, control,
and violence.

The letter to the Hebrews invites us to look at Jesus as a pioneer
and perfecter of our faith who endured such hostility against himself
from sinners (Heb 12:3). In Jesus the newness of God's love shines in
a human and vulnerable body. He is the one who doesn't love the
perfection, but the imperfection. Paradoxically his perfection is to
love fully the incompleteness of the world. In the middle of suffering and death he transforms them in new possibilities of life, in
resurrection.

What is sin if not a resistance, the unbelief of God's embracing love
who offers hospitality to the transience of the world? What is sin if
not our fear of mortality that moves us to grasp for the secure and
prevents us from being astonished, from inhabiting the body of the
world with passion? And is not our faith an exposure, an immersion,
a birth into God's loving waters that widen our hearts and attract us
in the adventure of an endless creation, where love outlives death?

God, in Jesus, interrupts the course of repetition, of violence, of
dominion, and opens a new potential direction: the ever-renewing

power of love stronger than the fears of death. Jesus expects the same prophetic fire that burns in him to burn also in his follower's heart, to transform the wounds into new life. "By each crime and every kindness, we birth our future."[1] Love perseveres through the storm, never giving up, always reaching out, and making space for something new to happen.

I came to bring fire to the Earth.

May we never underestimate our power of hope, the force to change the atmosphere around us, ignited by the flame of the divine and mysterious heart.

Note

1. *Cloud Atlas*, directed by Tom Tykwer, Andy Wachowski, and Lana Wachowski (Cloud Atlas Productions, 2012).

Twenty-Fourth Sunday in Ordinary Time

Exod 32:7-11, 13-14; 1 Tim 1:12-17; Luke 15:1-32

When I was studying theology, I was attracted by the harsh and magnetic poems of Paul Celan, a German-speaking Romanian Jew. One of his collections of poetry was titled *Atemwende, Breathturn*, evoking that elusive turning point, that single short moment when the in-breath reverses to the out-breath. Poetry, claims Celan, may be that *breathturn*, when a further "other" is set free, when the use of a word opens the door for other possible territories, for a fresh and unexpected meaning, for a revelation that was hidden, waiting to arise.

If to *sin* is to miss the mark, to get off the path, to turn into a deadlock, then all the stories that flavor our celebration today voice the experience of something missed or lost. At the same time they voice a breathturn that opens us to a new dimension, where a further "other" is set free: the fresh, surprising territory of grace. The Jewish people are called to a breathturn from worshiping a molten calf to a more subtle presence of the divine. They will experience a long and hard exodus through inhospitable places to learn that God is never an object to be found or possessed as we find other objects, even the golden ones.

In contrast, the Holy One shares our deepest subjectivity and relationality, asking for responsibility toward others, toward ourselves, and toward the spiritual reality of the Universe.

The apostle Paul acted ignorantly in unbelief but, he says, "the grace of the Holy One overflowed for me with faith and love that are in Christ Jesus." Paul spent all his life pursuing how to align the commandments of the law and God's will. He had built a strong, religious, and exclusive identity. All of a sudden he experienced his breathturn: he was blinded and was enlightened by a light coming from elsewhere that he calls "Christ."

Christ, the foolish love of God who knocks down every wall of separation, of distance, of darkness and shows us that our life is mysteriously hidden and woven in God, the source of joy. The Holy One sees the radiant Christ nature blazing through the facade of our human masks and creates a sacred space where that Divine Being within us—covered, buried, unknown, and disowned—can come forth and be fully seen, enjoyed, and embraced.

From this existential reversal Paul will toss out all things he once considered religiously essential. After Christ's death and resurrection, Paul is able to embrace and enjoy all cultural differences with the expanded heart of God's love that has now become his own new heart.

The youngest son of the gospel wanted to separate from his father and follow an imaginary fulfillment moved by his thirsts, desires, and hungers, as each of us is vulnerable to do. When we invest everything in something we think we can possess to satiate us, the object instead possesses us, blinds us, and we get lost. We can squander any energy we have but everything says to us, "I am not that for which you search."

Yet our disorientation, loss, and even disastrous mistakes can be the turning point that opens us to the intimacy of a truth that shines again and smiles on us. We awaken to a hidden Presence or Treasure that pulses at the heart of our soul, and yet we have lost it, we have failed to realize it, which is indeed the greatest of losses.

At the heart of evolution of matter, a creative potential that we call Christ is set free. It is no more the "I" that lives, with its depleting, contending, or competing drives, but Christ lives in me, the primal union with the source, the energy that propels us toward the target: a new creation in love.

Finally, how do we interpret this breathturn also from a planetary perspective? We are inhabitants of a planet threatened by climate change, degradation of soil, and loss of all natural resources thanks to our very choices and actions determined by a dominant and abusive relationship with nature. Like the prodigal son, we are squandering the tremendous inheritance built up in millions of years by Mother Earth! Are we willing to reconnect with the overflowing generosity of the Creator God? Will we consent to profoundly change our style of life, to be clothed by a new, healthy, and planetary awareness? To work out ways for us to get back to being the kind of beings we truly want to be, and the kind of society that is in accord with our own highest values and with the environmental needs of planet Earth?

> A pure heart create for me, O God,
> put a steadfast spirit within me.
> Do not cast me away from your presence,
> nor deprive me of your holy breath-turn.
> (see Ps 51:10-11, NRSV)

Twenty-Ninth Sunday in Ordinary Time

Exod 17:8-13; 2 Tim 3:14–4:2; Luke 18:1-8

In my musical wanderings I was surprised by the title that Aaron Parks, a young American jazz pianist, gave to his last composition: *Arborescence.* Arborescence is a word for the way something grows—seeking and adaptive—like a tree with its roots, or with its branches moving under and around things wherever they need to go to find water and sun. For Aaron Parks the pieces of his album's music developed as if they were coming into being and going where they had to go, in that sort of arboreal way.

The posture of Moses, standing on the top of the hill with his hands held up toward the source of Life, reminds me of this arborescence way of being: a tree with open branches, its leaves exposed to the Sun's light. Moses' pose evokes *a tree of prayer*, an arboreal way of existence, the movement of life outstretched toward a source in whom to place our confidence and hope.

Moses' arboreal embodiment reveals that perhaps prayer precedes us humans: that we are a conscious and worshiping variation of the many ways Earth has found to expose herself to light to unfurl and grow. Photosynthesis is the primal way Earth has invented to receive and to be nourished by the radiating solar source, and her adaptive response has created an intimate bond between herself and the Sun. Earth's life totally depends now on the powerful energy of Sun's light, and she lifts up her perennial worship in receiving and transforming the superabundant gift of light. The ramified gesture of Moses, hands held up from dawn to dusk, reminds us of the persistent, insistent, always praying prayer of the Earth coming into being, open to receive the promising gift of light.

We are invited by today's liturgy to celebrate, to sense, to expand this prayer of the Universe, of Earth, unfurling from the big bang to the groaning labor pains of our global humanity, the universal Body of Christ. Jesus represents a breakthrough moment in this immense tree of prayer. With him the Sun's radiance can be received as love and finds tangible expression in history. Through his body he is able to transform revenge into forgiveness, fear into trust, violence into peace, exclusion into inclusion, brokenness into healing, and death into new life.

We have been grafted into the new consciousness of Jesus that transforms the light's radiance into an encompassing love in a way that nourishes us and those around us. In our planetary age we no more pray to win an enemy in war, but our prayer opens in other directions, toward hunting ghosts that we ourselves have created in our global culture. Our hands are held up toward the Generative Womb asking for a deep change of our systematic and ongoing destruction of the sources of life on Earth.

Some young students in their house garage have invented a bacterium that eats plastic and exudes a kind of diesel: it is their ecological prayer. They have been enkindled by the passion of sustainability, seeking a way to turn destruction into a creative and adaptive response to the threats to our planet.

Today our hands and hearts are held up, asking justice, health, and democracy for so many people that are beneath the weight of oppression and exclusion. This Sunday urges us to persevere in prayer because the essential elements we pray or struggle for—love, health, justice, democracy—are not there, but are *coming*; they are unfulfilled promises; they persistently press in upon our present, refusing to content itself, open to an uncontainability of life to come.

And yet, when the Son of humanity comes, will he find faith on Earth?

In our persistent cry we voice the insistent Mystery from the inside of creation. Surprisingly enough, the name of God is not what appeases us but disturbs and upsets us like the bothering widow of the gospel. Is not the Holy One the insistent knocking, inside of us and through us? It is the knocking at the door of our mind, heart, and consciousness to continue God's transforming action and self-giving. It is the passionate knocking at the door of our social, political, economic, or religious systems to enhance life. In fact, if there is nothing in our life to cry about, if there is nothing in our life to yell about, we must be out of touch and out of love.

> You are Mystery of knocking, cry, and openness
> in our silent and fiery prayer,
> breath and light rippling through our innermost recesses.
> You are sorrow in the most tender spots of our existence
> eager to ramify through, and beyond them
> into wings of resurrection, and joy.

Thirty-Second Sunday in Ordinary Time

2 Macc 7:1-2, 9-14; 2 Thess 2:16–3:5; Luke 20:27, 34-38

Instead of the gruesome scene of the Maccabees in the first reading, or the ludicrous account of the Sadducees in the gospel, let us follow the path of the stars!

Lawrence Krauss, a renowned cosmologist, ironically claimed in a lecture, "Every atom in your body came from a star that exploded. . . . So, forget Jesus. The stars died so that you could be here today." We have discovered that the final stages of stars called *supernova* are an event of death and dissolution in favor of life. They explode, disseminating their hot fragments in space, giving birth to new forms of being. It appears that our solar system originated from these scattered fragments of a supernova explosion in the Milky Way. Together with interstellar dust and the influence of gravity, the Sun began to form, and then planets began to orbit around the Sun, and Earth appeared, and various life forms, and at last we humans emerged. "The massive star that was mother to our Sun met with a fiery death, her form completely annihilated by the explosive force of the blast. And yet she exists in each one of us, in the cells of our bodies that are composed of her dust."[1]

It seems that this pattern of dissolution, through which new and creative manifestations emerge, deeply permeates the web of life. And that the mystery of death and resurrection is inscribed in the very DNA of the Universe, in the cosmic scale, which is how God transforms reality, creates, and gives birth to newness. Jesus is our morning star, embodied brightness of boundless Love. In the paschal

mystery he accepts with consciousness and freedom the coming
Passover, which has been prepared by many episodes of dying.
Throughout his journey Jesus experienced the increasing hostility of
religious authorities, withdrawal of people, misunderstanding of the
disciples, betrayal of Judas, and the disavowal of Peter. He experienced the death of his relationship with his mother and friends, and
the dissolution of his dream of grace on Earth that he called reign of
God. He suffered the death of being cut off from Love itself in his cry
of abandonment addressed to his Abba. We could include in his death
also the betrayals and disavowals of his good news throughout the
ensuing centuries of Christianity.

Jesus went through all these multifaceted deaths in a contemplative journey, continually watered by the divine Wellspring of his life.
Jesus addresses, absorbs, and transforms all that is not life-giving, all
that limits the expansion of creative love that can happen in this world
and within our life. "Each of these little dyings—as Judy Cannato
writes—releases the Spirit, and a lifetime of such choices manifests
a spiritual power that cannot be defeated by death, not even death
on a cross."[2] In his violent execution he is a supernova explosion of
divine compassion at the heart of our limitations and resistances,
within the sinful condition of this world. Going through the violent
and dark night of the world, Jesus reveals that by so entering these
depths, the Spirit of God opens the promise of unpredictable life
through and beyond death.

In the midst of our pains, anxieties, and deaths, Jesus opens the
eyes of our heart revealing God at work *there*, widening the doors of
our limited perceptions. He enkindles our faith in the possibility of
resurrection. Through us the Spirit of Christ continues to transform
death into life. Sandra Schneiders, in her thin and dense meditation
titled *The Resurrection*, asserts, "During the Paschal event Jesus's
bodily return takes up his indwelling presence within and among
his disciples, flooding them with his nearness, his presence, his intimacy, and is no longer subject to the constraints of time and space,
and the ordinary laws of causality."[3]

This Sunday we celebrate the overflowing of the Living God within
our constraints, limited measurements, exclusions, and impossibili-
ties. We celebrate this event with some lines from Julie Cadwallader
Staub's poem "Measurement":[4]

Look at us:
we quantify everything we can
in this complex and astonishing world,

. . . .

But no one can measure the velocity of hope,
the way hope hatches
     fully fledged—in fact, already flying—
     between one word and the next
     between one breath and the next.

. . . .

And we can only try to imagine the circumference of compassion
the way it shows us the shape of love
     embracing, expanding,
     factoring in forgiveness
     it invents its own quantum leap,
     its own speed of light.

Notes

1. Judy Cannato, *Radical Amazement: Contemplative Lessons from Black Holes, Supernovas, and Other Wonders of the Universe* (Notre Dame, IN: Sorin, 2006), 119–20.

2. Ibid., 122.

3. Sandra M. Schneiders, *The Resurrection: Did It Really Happen and Why Does That Matter?* (Los Angeles: Marymount Institute Press, 2013), 36.

4. Julie Cadwallader Staub, "Measurement," *Spiritus* 13, no. 1 (Spring 2013): 120.

Perspectives on Eco-Spirituality

Intertwining Gospel and Ecology

*The same stream of life that runs through my veins night and day
runs through the world and dances in rhythmic measures.*

—Rabindranath Tagore

In the middle of the global, planetary crisis that we are living, our
reflection tries to find inspiration, wisdom, and a contemplative mind
from our Christian sources. How can we interpret, envision, and
embody our faith in the present moment of history when we seem
to once again be going through a narrow, dramatic passage on the
journey of the Universe and of our planet Earth?

Our epoch seems to be a *jump time* where something is collapsing
and something new is emerging. Is this a new stage of our evolutionary exodus that involves participation and responsibility, urging us
to become cocreators with the all-nourishing Mystery of life?

This environmental, social, and spiritual crisis asks that we give
careful consideration and attention to the natural world in its own
right, from its own perspective, so that our spirituality may be
grounded deeply in creation dynamics, in the journey of the Universe.
"There is a great book," writes Saint Augustine, "the book of created
nature. God did not make letters of ink for you to recognize him in;
he set before your eyes all these things he has made. . . . Heaven
and Earth cries out to you, 'God made me.'"[1]

I will present some perspectives on a spirituality that is connected with our Earth, with the natural world of life—an *eco-spirituality*. We will orbit around four images inspired from the New Testament.

1. Coming Back/Forward to Life
(The salvific turn: Luke 15:11-24)

We begin with an excerpt from Christopher Fry's *A Sleep of Prisoners*:[2]

> Dark and cold we may be, but this
> Is no winter now. The frozen misery
> Of centuries, cracks, begins to move,
> The thunder is the thunder of the floes,
> The thaw, the flood, the upstart Spring.
> Thank God our time is now when wrong
> Comes up to face us everywhere,
> Never to leave us till we take
> The longest stride of soul [humans] ever took.
> Affairs are now soul size.
> The enterprize
> Is exploration into God.

According to the poet, we are living times of breaks, cracks, and demises; yet they are not just the end, rather the flood of an "upstart Spring," where the size of the problems reach down into the deep places of the human mind and heart, of our collective consciousness and behaviors. Finally, it is an exploration into God, the hidden heart of the Cosmos, the Mystery of the world.

In the context of our ecological crisis and of a correspondent eco-spirituality, I find it extraordinarily challenging and interesting to reinterpret the parable of the squandering son that we find in the Gospel of Luke. Rather than the individual perspective that we are used to, let's look at the risky situation we are collectively living today on our planet Earth.

We approach this story as a provocative call for a Great Turning[3] within the collapse of industrial civilization, and the transformation of our relationship with the Earth, our home and source of life, and with the divine, all-nourishing Source.

Just as the prodigal son, requesting his part of the inheritance, decided to leave the paternal house and squandered all his goods through a debauched life—so our society and Western culture (which has become a global culture) are squandering our inheritance through the way we live. We have *separated* from the Earth out of which we are born and from which we derive all that we are and all that we have, depleting by our choices and actions all the natural resources created over billions of years by extraordinary and complex processes of life.

As the prodigal son came close to a threat of death that urged him to awaken, to make a deep shift, and to move back/forward to the source of life, into a gift economy—so our epoch is pressed into a jump time by the impending danger of a common extinction. In the face of collapse we may awake to *a new planetary consciousness*, to establish a new relationship with the Earth, our home, and be able to transform with a different worldview our choices and lifestyles. How can this alienation from the Earth and the consequent environmental crisis have happened?

In the first place we express our appreciation for the great, complex, powerful event that we call *modernity* that has characterized our Western civilization. Approximately four hundred years ago the planet Earth awakened to a new intellectual, scientific understanding of itself. We reached a new level of consciousness, a capacity to intensify our power of attention and to transform reality. Thanks to our instruments and calculations, which are expansions of our bodies, we were able to go beyond nature and to predict the movements of the planets and the *laws* of matter. We transformed all this knowledge into the wonderful power of machines in order to satisfy our human needs and desires. Earth and nature have always been our allies and opponents; we have always tried to overstep the constraints of our biological limitedness. The technological revolution has allowed us to plan and to build, to cure and to produce. This enormous power has gradually replaced the selective processes of nature, allowing us to intervene and to modify the structures of life, to mold the external world according to a project and a technique.

"Modern industrial humans broke with the past. They did not seek to commune with nature or to revere it as divine gift. They sought to transform the world. For they had a dream. Using these new technological powers, they would create a better world, one with greater quantities of food, more efficient transportation, and faster communication. Using their new machines, they would eliminate poverty, hunger, and sickness."[4] They refused to just wait for a heavenly reality elsewhere, and they wanted to build heaven here on Earth. What seemed the wonderful enterprise of civilization has created at the same time our crisis: we are paying a high cost in a gradual voiding of intelligence, wisdom, soul, beauty, spirit, meaning, purpose, and love from the entire world.

I will try now to mention *some main features* that have molded the structures of our Western mind, myth, narrative, belief systems, and collective imagination and have guided us to dire straits. From the dawn of the sixteenth century we detect the emergence of an instrumental and assuring *reason*, a *rational mind* based on an objectifying *separation* between human beings and the rest of the Earth.

At the beginning of the scientific enterprise there is an approach to reality based on the ability to measure matter as mere *quantity*. The Universe and the Earth were considered as extended, passive, raw, and inert material, a substance devoid of subjectivity. They were considered *vast machines* subject to the mechanical laws that we discover at work in them, and that we can use to our own advantage. Moving away from nature, we made ourselves the center, with the world orbiting around us, handling it as simple stuff to exploit and to consume for our interests and goals. Matter now exists primarily for human use, a worldview that provides a rationale for the "global economy of corporate capitalism" dismantling Earth's ecosystems.[5]

We have increasingly amplified our control and action on the Earth, altering the very functioning of the atmosphere and biosphere. The survival of the species of ecosystems now depends primarily on human activity. We have become a *geophysical force*: we have entered into an era shaped primarily by humans. "Our progressive ownership of the world naturally and inevitably accompanies our progressive estrangement from the world."[6]

This conquering project, the dream of the industrial age for an infinite material growth and expansion, is collapsing under our eyes: the oceans, the rivers, the atmosphere, and the soil have all been severely degraded by our actions and choices. The money system has contributed to competition, poverty, and scarcity, and it has destroyed species, communities, and cultures. The converging crises of energy, environment, and economics characterize the end of industrial civilization. Yet, trouble, crisis, demise, danger, fear, and risk are all part of the evolutionary world we inhabit, representing a favorable and maybe a necessary opportunity for a shift. We have the chance to go inward, to the resources of the soul, and we have a chance to learn the world again, to be catalyst of a new pattern of evolution.

As the parable of the prodigal son teaches us, God's agency is particularly at work in the moment of despair, in the dark nights of history: the collapse may become a *spiritual* reality, a journey of transformation through which all of us at this turn of history must pass. We are going through a necessary evolutionary trauma in the journey of the planet Earth.[7]

We are aware that new economics paradigms are emerging, like micro-credit, local currencies, and gift economies. Restorative justice is growing, focusing on the needs of the victims and the offenders as well as the involved community. New technological solutions or green alternatives are developing, like solar power, wind power, bio-diesel. Permaculture principles are developing for designing gardens, building homes, and using land.

Authors like Jacob Needleman, Carolyn Becker, and others invite us to interpret the ecological crisis not only as a technological problem but as an expression of a spiritual crisis, encompassing all aspects of our humanity, reaching down into the deep places of our human mind, heart, dream vision, purpose, unspoken beliefs that shape our consciousness and behavior.

Our return back is in fact a going *forward*, beyond our previous story and behavior of separation, sovereignty, and conquest. The journey leads us home to a place we see anew, because the Universe and Earth are still coming into bloom: it is toward the world's future that we are drawn. Our conversion involves a new heart of care and mutuality, *a sense of intimacy* with the Earth and all sentient beings, especially now that we have come to know our history of the Universe, the innumerable and amazing transformations that have happened to the Universe until the Earth found expression, and how our humanity is inseparable from the materiality and spirituality of the planet.

We take *responsibility* for all creatures to whom we owe a debt of gratitude, because we have become what we are thanks to all of them. We meet the divine Mystery in the flesh of the world, taking care of the Earth, of all living forms, of those who have appeared, of those who are oppressed, of the indigenous cultures and spirituality that have been destroyed, and of those who will come. What we need is a new experience of Earth not as an inert and static object but a sentient being, a "sensuous body":[8] we allow the world itself to have a soul and an interior life.

For the prodigal son the journey led to an unexpected abundance of grace, to a shared, gratuitous banquet of joy, delight, and a new relationship with the Father. Like the prodigal son, we are also transformed in our view of God: from a despotic, hierarchical, and sovereign image of God Almighty to a Father/Mother who is a source of generosity, creative forgiveness, empowering us to continue God's caretaking, generosity, and sharing. The parable blossoms in a eucharistic banquet of divine abundance, the gift of waters and air, of dawn and sunsets, of birds and trees, of the music of Mozart and the songs of Beyoncé, and of all the wisdoms and cultures of the world.

Liberated from constricted notions of who we are and what we need, we are brought to a banquet where we share the goods that are common with gratitude and thanksgiving. We share an inclusive community, integrity of the earth, peace and justice, which we can accomplish in "communion" with others, developing the gifts of technology in service of the Earth.

Despair taught the son to embark on a journey back/forward to home: What is despair teaching us? What are we learning from the demise of the narrative of separation? What is the de-industrial future, the next culture we humans have the opportunity to create? Can our faith communities become spaces where we experience and celebrate an eco-spirituality coming back/forward to a relationship with the Earth that is no longer exploitative and indifferent, but appreciative for the richness of the divine presence in matter, the Earth as an embodiment of God's generosity and passion?

The choice is ours: to become a healing or a deleterious presence on the planet.

2. A Regenerative Baptism (Matt 3:16-17)

We approach a second aspect beginning with Julie Cadwallader Staub's "Measurement":[9]

Look at us:
we quantify everything we can
in this complex and astonishing world,
from nanoseconds to eons
from millimeters to miles
from basis points to billions.

But no one can measure the velocity of hope,
the way hope hatches
     fully fledged—in fact, already flying—
     between one word and the next
     between one breath and the next.

Neither can we calculate the stain of fear,
the way it infects a childhood
     spreads to a lifetime.

And we can only try to imagine the circumference of compassion
the way it shows us the shape of love
     embracing, expanding,
     factoring in forgiveness
     it invents its own quantum leap,
     its own speed of light.

    The poet suggests that for our desire of grasping the magnitude of the world we reduce it to our measurements. Today our knowledge is often identified with the precision and efficacy of our measurements: we have defined ourselves "measure of all things." However, our increasing desire to quantify has become a cage, a trap, a destructive circle where every common good is pressed into servitude, treated as a resource to use, to be owned, bought, and sold.

    Yet there are sizes and scales that exceed our most sophisticated unit of measurement and evaluation. The poet mentions hope and compassion; we could add beauty and imagination, or joy, justice, and faith, not to mention the exuberant vitality of our planet and cosmic life, and the unfathomable divine action. Following the invitation of the poet, we want to move toward different qualities of measurements, of perceptions.

We yearn for a *regenerative baptism* of our minds and hearts, of our destructive and consumptive behaviors.

I invite you to widen cosmically the experience of the baptism of Jesus as an experience that embraces all of us in this birthing that enfolds the Universe in all its forms.

As the baptism was for Jesus a transformative event, a widening of measurements, of consciousness, so for us it means a plunging into a reality larger than ourselves, into the deep waters of Earth, Cosmos, and Spirit. And we emerge transformed, resurrected to a new vision of Earth and Cosmos as the indwelling, sacramental presence of the Divine.

Let us pause and consider the rich, deep, and active elements that are present in the scene of the gospel. There are welcoming waters, heavens that are opened, a human immersion and emersion, a descending Spirit, a mysterious and passionate voice: "You are my beloved."

The waters are pools of life. On Earth, both plant and animal life were born in the primordial seas, some three billion years ago. The fundamental structures of our bodies developed from fish. In the waters we trace the early stages in the history of our skulls, necks, lungs, and limbs. Inside every organ, cell, and piece of DNA of our bodies lie over 3.5 billion years of the history of life. In his book *The Hero's Journey*, the comparative mythologist Joseph Campbell says, "Almost every mythology that knows anything about water sees the origins of life coming out of water. . . . and then again, finally, in science, we find the same thing."[10]

Indeed, our scientific discoveries have shown that our story plunges into more deep waters than the sea; it sinks into the cosmic ocean. The Earth process itself was born out of the solar system, and out of heavens beyond the solar system: It is in the explosions of stars that the primordial elements took shape. Out of those elements the solar system and Earth were born, and the oceans, and from single-celled creatures all species of sentient beings, and our human bodies, with brains so richly textured that allow us self-reflection, freedom, and love.

In the prologue to *The Universe Within*, the biological scientist Neil Shubin writes, "Worms, fish, and algae are but gateways to ever deeper connections—ones that extend back billions of years before

the presence of life and of Earth itself. Written inside us is the birth
of the stars, the movement of heavenly bodies across the sky, even
the origin of days themselves. . . . Within each of us lie some of the
most profound stories of all."[11]

Imagine the feeling of immensity sensed by the astronomer Edwin
Hubble when, using the Hooker telescope on Mount Wilson, he discovered a multitude of creative galaxies existing beyond our Milky
Way galaxy, thought to be the only existing one. Even more astonishing, he discovered that new space is coming into being as the Universe continues to endlessly expand outward in all directions. The
heavens embed us into a creative, mysterious, and evolutionary
Cosmos, which emerged as a whole over billions of years of creative
processes.

Thomas Berry, historian of world religions and cultures, says, "The
universe, the solar system, and the planet Earth in themselves and
in their evolutionary emergence constitute for the human community
the primary revelation of that mystery whence all things came into
being."[12] We have finally realized that the Earth is a living organism,
that the whole planetary world is alive. Our modern knowledge
reveals a Universe with a psychic-spiritual dimension from the beginning: It is a self-aware creative process, permeated by self-organizing
dynamics and complex patterns, which is ultimately mysterious. And
it expresses beauty and elegance, purpose and meaning. Finally, Earth
herself begins her adventure of conscious self-awareness with human
consciousness. The Universe, Earth, the immense chorus of creatures,
and our symbolic consciousness reveal unfathomable depths and
heights. There are uncountable layers of creative waters, of open
heavens; there are levels of matter, soul, and spirit, of imagination
and creativity, of transmaterial dimensions and energies.

All creation is the flowering of deeply cosmic energies, where the
visible is interwoven with the invisible (dark matter and dark energy
constitute 95 percent of the Universe and are unseen). There is a
hidden heart of Cosmos. What is that invisible, elusive element that
opens the heavens of the journey of the Universe, of our planet Earth,
of our personal and communal experience?

We are invited by many authors to rediscover the cosmic presence
and action of the *creative Spirit*, of holy Sophia (see Prov 8:22-31), from
the beginning of the journey throughout the natural world unto the

end. According to Elizabeth A. Johnson and Kathleen Duffy, the Spirit-Sophia pervades the material world with graceful vigor and life-giving power, holding all things together. It is God's own Spirit who blossoms forth, breathes life into the chaos, agglomerates, quickens, groans in labor pains, dismantles, renews, sets free unknown potentialities, blesses, continuously creates—bringing forth this exuberant, expanding, and unfinished Universe.[13]

We perceive the mysterious action of this loving God as an inspiring power that dwells at the heart of Cosmos, sustaining every stage of its emergence and complexity. Considered in the continuous radiance of this self-giving presence, world and Earth are not separated from their sacred source, are not just considered instrumental to humans' concern and need, but put on instead a sacramental character: All of nature is embraced and nourished by the divine presence, and Earth from her origin has an intrinsic spiritual quality. Matter is fecund, alive, interconnected, permeated by the presence of the Spirit at play in creation, and we are called to witness and to praise the God who is "above all and through all and in all" (Eph 4:6).

We celebrate the radical incarnation and baptism of "God who is situated within every speck of matter . . . and who is beyond the world as the unseen source of all that we experience."[14] We acknowledge the Spirit as unending creativity that created us, and is all around us, and endows the Universe with the capacity to transcend its acquired forms into new meanings, values, shapes, manifestations, new capacities of freedom and love. We consent to a Spirit who is pulling forward on the direction of the not yet, of an unperfected Universe that implies suffering and love.

In the gospels, the peak of the baptismal experience is a voice that comes from the hidden heart of the Holy, addressed to Jesus: *you are my beloved* embodiment. It is a voice reminiscent of the Song of Songs: *A voice, my beloved* (Song 2:8), and of the pleased voice that at the beginning of creation repeatedly exclaims, *It is good, it is very good* (Gen 1:1-31).

In a meaningful gesture, Jesus plunges into the height and the abyss of our humanity and of creation to embrace them all, to relate heaven and heart, matter and life, body and mind within himself, and in so doing roots himself in the Power that created his special human freedom.

Totally grasped by the divine Eros, Jesus bathes in the fiery waters of matter, plunges into Earth where it is deepest and most violent, to struggle in its current dedicating himself to transform the Cosmos to a new level of consciousness and love. He passes through the constraining walls of our bodies, souls, and cultures: walls raised by fears and cemented by violence, injustice, and exclusions. He crosses the hardened places of our hearts, our brokenness, agony, and despairs. Jesus is the cosmic, *emergent Christ*. According to Ilia Delio, the Christ that appeared in the body of Jesus is not confined there; he is still emerging in the body of the world as God's scandalous, radical, revolutionary, unconditional love.[15] He continues the ongoing process of crumbling down the walls that block the infinite light hidden in God's heart and creation, continually nourishing meaning, hope, and faith. An uprising of love, attracting us out of the tomb toward an unfurling fullness of love that supports everything, is still ripe, and is not finished yet.

In our time we plunge into a new, dramatic baptism of human evolution. An openness is needed to see: a new level of consciousness and care is required in this moment in which we are destroying our Earth. Is it possible that the immense journey of the Universe and of the spirit blossoming in our human consciousness will lead to destruction? Or are we presenting our personal and communal bodies not conformed to the exploitative logic of this world (Rom 12:1-2) but for the birth on earth of the divine element, for a vision of wholeness, for an action of inclusion of all planet Earth?

3. In the Beginning, the Relationship (John 1:1-5, 14)

We introduce ourselves into the third perspective, listening to a verse of the poem "Spirit of Love" by Barbara Deming:[16]

> Our own pulse beats in every stranger's throat,
> And also there within the flowered ground beneath our feet;
> And—teach us to listen!—
> We can hear it in water, in wood, and even in stone.
> We are earth of this earth, and we are bone of its bone.
> This is a prayer I sing, for we have forgotten this and so
> The earth is perishing.

"We are earth of this earth, and we are bone of its bone," the poet sings—pointing to our belonging to the body of the planet, living threads interwoven in the tapestry of Earth, the beating of her heart beating in the heart of each one of us and of all creatures.

There is a breathtaking icon of this deep, amazing, and radical unity of the planet. From the spacecraft Apollo we could contemplate our Earth from outside for the first time: a tiny planet, an incredibly rare jewel of a blue marble floating in a black ocean of space in all its beauty, wholeness, diversity, and aliveness.

I invite you to appreciate, celebrate, and sense this connected wholeness of our Earth in the light of the first verses of the prologue of John's gospel:

> *In the beginning was the living Word, a Word sharing oneness with God.*
> *All things are coming into being through this creative Word*
> *that will become flesh, human-divine consciousness and love.*

We can be caught in the wreckage of financial, ecological, and communicative crises. We have raised walls of separation and incommunicability; we have spread consumptive behaviors, rugged individualism, and meaningless fragmentation, so that the Earth and our industrial civilization are perishing. Yet, John's gospel reminds us of a *life-giving* and *life-connecting* Word that continues to be uttered and has the potential to reconnect us with what matters most: the holiness of our heart, the heart of holiness beating at the heart of each one of us, of all creatures, and of the Cosmos.

The Word, the creative energy of the Holy One, is the hidden agent, the unifying heart of Cosmos, weaving the texture of reality in greater complexity, freedom, and consciousness, in the unity of love that is creation itself. *Connectedness* and *interconnection* are the expressions that better evoke the action of this Word in the world. The Universe, as we now know, unfolded from a hot point, from a common cosmic source, an initial free and creative event, particles of matter and light expanding in an endless adventure. We have been suffused with and accompanied by light since the beginning of time through a very long, winding, and risky journey.

Our scientific instruments allow us to realize that, from the beginning, forms of communication, connection, and friendship shaped the emerging Cosmos: gravitational, nuclear, and electromagnetic interactions connect nuclei, atoms, and molecules; conglomerate galaxies, planets, cells, and organisms. We contemplate at best the blossoming, the symphony of interconnection in our planet Earth, in its embracing atmosphere, in its magnificent web of life where everything is inscribed in a richly interwoven network.

Turning our attention to the bodies of creatures and to our own bodies, we discover an elegant and refined composition of organs and interactive senses we have inherited and developed from other species. We are detecting that the texture of our brains is the most complex and interconnected expression of life we know. We have realized that we are made by the same matter that radiated from the big bang, and that we share the same DNA of all sentient beings. We may perceive ourselves as part or ripple of the immense wave of life, and we breathe together the same air that connects our own bodies with the body of all living creatures and Mother Earth.

Is it not the same movement of connection that we can detect in animals' passions? By their very nature, passions drive us to go out of a self toward another, and they intensify during evolution, shifting from a medium of reproduction and survival of the species toward greater eros, intimacy, union, pleasure, care, and self-giving behavior. "There is little validity to the idea that humans are isolated individuals, for each of us arises out of an ocean of experience and understanding acquired by our species as a whole, . . . participat[ing] in a collective process."[17]

A radical new view of human nature is emerging. The biological and cognitive sciences are forcing us to rethink the belief that human beings are, by nature, aggressive, materialistic, utilitarian, and self-interested. We are a fundamentally *empathic species*,[18] and it is our cooperative social interaction that engendered our cognitive uniqueness, our symbolic consciousness. It is this communicative interaction with humans and nonhuman beings that has led us to the present global consciousness,[19] where the world is unified and related by instruments of communication that we have created as an expansion of our bodies.

Many persons perceive that we are entering into a new phase of evolution, where the Earth is connected by a global nervous system that we are creating. The Jesuit paleontologist Pierre Teilhard de Chardin created the word *noosphere* to express a connective mind or consciousness that embraces all the planet. The evolutionary pioneer

Barbara Marx Hubbard imagines and experiences the next stage of our evolution as a shift of our species from Me, to We, to New Whole, from *Homo sapiens sapiens* to *Homo universalis.*

All these worldviews are saying that natural and human history is moving toward an increasing connection, unity, and consciousness, toward endlessly linking systems without closure. We can say that all matter is energy in relationship, and that the Cosmos is a participatory Universe.

According to many authors, from Ken Wilber to Rupert Sheldrake, Judy Cannato, and Ilia Delio, the journey of the Universe is teaching us that creation emerges with evolution as lower-level entities become higher-level entities; parts enter in communion with a greater whole through the gradual unification of multiplicity, where, for example, an atom is part of a whole molecule, and a molecule is part of a whole cell, and a cell is part of a whole organ, and an organ is part of a whole organism. Each whole depends on all the other wholes below it to maintain its own being and is an essential component of the larger whole: everyone and everything is connected to everything and everyone else. Earth is a whole made of parts; our solar system is a whole made of parts; all wholes are part of something more complex and all are contained in the one Universe that is home to all.

Given this fundamental interconnectedness, this field of communion, if we destroy or pollute Earth's delicate balance in one of its parts, be it air, water, soil, or species, the result is an action of destruction not only for human beings but also for all other living creatures. We breathe together, we all share the same air, and that connects us with every sentient being. We weave a web in which our energies, our creations, and our insights can circulate.

We are woven by the life-giving, relational Word and Spirit. The interconnectedness of our expanding Universe mirrors a *God as a mystery of relationship,* and this relationship is profoundly and essentially *love.* In our Christian tradition we name this divine, threefold relationship of love *Trinity.* We are invited by faith to enter into this virtuous and expanding circle of communication where there is no uniformity and exclusion, but dynamism of outpouring and receiving.

We believe in an all-embracing Mystery who is not monolithic or domineering but relational Source in itself, promoting relationship and union of differences in a more complex reality. This empathic dance of love is seeking and creating connection, moving toward greater consciousness and communion through the deep, cosmic time of evolution.

As Ilia Delio claims, "God participates in creation because God is dynamic, relational being whose openness to relationship is the basis of evolution."[20] Love by its nature is creative union; it is the divine Energy of creation, the Spirit hovering over all processes of evolving life, and the incarnation of God's compassionate yearning.

John's prologue, with boldness, nerve, and unbridled imagination, joins the creative energy of God's word, through whom the Universe continues to unfurl, to the human and messy embodiment of Jesus Christ, manifestation of God's glory, imprint of God's being. The infinite light that is birthing the Cosmos has generated a receptive body, a point of conjunction of light and love, of human and divine that is a historical being: Jesus, a vulnerable, contestable, disposable body, an exposed and begging Word that creatively embraces the glories and humiliations of the flesh.

Jesus is for us the exemplar, the *mirror of relatedness*: he promotes wholeness toward God: he embodies a radical unity with the Holy One, with humans, and with the entire groaning creation; he is able to embrace even the enemy, the destructor, and death. And he wants that same radical unity, togetherness, to define those who follow him: "that they may be one, as we are one" (John 17:11-22).

The new Universe story as a relatedness network, as an interwoven whole of wholes, invites us to promote a *spirituality of connectedness*, and to expand our heart to include all expressions of creation. Seeing the ways in which all of life is connected, we are called to a conversion of consciousness: from an anthropocentric and dominating vision of the world, where we are separated from the rest, and the center of all, to an *eco-centric* vision of the Universe, where we are reintegrated back into the ecosystem.

We are called to a different kind of relationship with what surrounds us: an interactive, responsible, sympathetic, empathic, and co-creative *dialogue* with the Earth. This relational vision of the Universe invites us to become ministers of integration, *bridging agents*: between mind, body, and spirit; heaven and earth; feminine and masculine; big and small; past and present; science and religion; humans and nonhumans—animals and technologies; among classes, races, ages, genders, cultures, and religions.

We are invited by this new vision of our connectedness to rethink and to embody the meaning of "catholicity" as *openness* in contrast to what is partial, sectarian, exclusive, or selective.[21] The emergence of a catholic dimension implies a dynamism of inclusion and universality that transcends every closure and separation; it evokes an ungraspable mystery of fullness that attracts us toward a promising future. Maybe, to become, to grow catholic as being-in-connectedness means to have care of wholeness, to incarnate a *liturgy of hospitality* where the church is a house for all, a field of togetherness, of mutual enhancement, compassion, and friendship. And are not the sacraments the junction, insertion, joint, and connection of our littleness, of our partiality into the infinite vastness of God's love and wholeness, so that the Ultimate Reality can be all in all?

4. **The Groaning of Creation** (Rom 8:22-24)

We listen to a provocative poem by Rebecca del Rio, "Constant":[22]

> The constant is this:
> life is chaos, disintegration, blooming
> anew into order and collapsing
> again to blossom into something perfect,
> then chaos, disintegration and on.
>
> We watch helplessly, entranced
> like the magician's audience,
> the hypnotist's mark.
>
> Nothing to do but join hands,
> bow heads, say blessings
> to the capricious, wild
> original god.

This poem reminds us that the immense and unfinished journey of the Universe, including all the stages of matter, life, and human emergence, is not only characterized by growth, blossoming, and beauty, but is crossed and exposed to chaos, suffering, disintegration, and death. "The fact of the matter is that glorious life arises and is renewed in the midst of its perpetual perishing. Biologically, pain and death accompany the ongoing passage of life."[23]

According to the powerful image of Paul in his letter to the Romans, the whole creation has been groaning in labor pains until now, like a woman in childbirth, like a cosmic womb straining toward a future of fruitfulness (Rom 8:22-24), and in the midst we participate in what John F. Haught calls "the transformative drama of life."[24] We are still in a process of becoming, drawn by a future of promise, open to unpredictability, risk, and newness, and infused by God's grace.

> The constant is this:
> life is chaos, disintegration, blooming anew.

The texture of the Universe is permeated by violence, pain, and demise; it embraces both creativity and destruction, life and death, collapse and emergence of novelty, joy and suffering—all intertwined into the very womb of the Universe. And yet, with hopeful good news, Paul reminds us that within the crucible of cosmic, biological, and human struggle the Spirit ferments, enhances, connects, and is birthing, making life grow through death.

Listening carefully to the story of evolution, we learn that creatures are the result of billions of years of a meandering, contingent, and haphazard process marked by untold pain, failed attempts, and enormous waste. As Brian Thomas Swimme tells it, "The Universe throughout space and time is filled with violence and chaos. Millions of galaxies have been destroyed; trillions of animals have been killed" in mass extinctions, ice ages, earthquakes, and erupting volcanoes, without counting predation, human violence, and our present devastation of the environment.[25] With pain and suffering, death also is a paradoxical presence that allows the unfolding of life. As Judy Cannato reminds us, "The massive star that was mother to our Sun met with fiery death, her form completely annihilated by the explosive force of the blast. And yet she exists in each one of us, in the cells of our bodies that are composed of her dust. We are her children for whom she sacrificed all. Our bodies are issues of solar, galactic, and cosmic stuff. We are forged from stardust, from earth, wind, water, from all the animal species that have shaped our environment, and our bodies."[26] More specifically, paying attention to how animal and human organs developed, death has been a "necessary" element for the shaping of our senses, passions, and brains, as the multitude of deaths has favored complexity, diversity, exploration and the unfolding of new forms of life.

This commingling of life and death in favor of life that seems to be inscribed in the DNA of the Universe encourages us not to separate these elements, but to consider them as a constant to the labor and adventure of life. Our faith believes that the unfolding of life is embraced by God shining in the flesh of a situated creature: Jesus Christ. In him the cosmic and biological groaning of creation, the incessant striving of life is embodied and opened to a future of grace, liberation, and promise. "Understood theologically, what is *really* going on in evolution is that the whole creation, as anticipated by the incarnation and resurrection of Christ, is being transformed into the bodily abode of God."[27]

In the paschal mystery of death and resurrection, Jesus enters his violent and iniquitous death, placing his trust in the hands of the beloved and all-embracing Source that inspired and nourished all the passionate and life-giving actions of his existence. Every time Jesus touches limitations, wounds, boundaries, oppositions, and exclusions of his time and culture there is a release of the creative Spirit, a foretaste of liberation, of resurrection, an opening to a fullness of life that we call God. "The cross reveals to us the heart of God because it reveals the vulnerability of God's love."[28]

In the event of resurrection Jesus enters the eternal life of Love, carrying with him the groaning, yearning, and hope of the evolutionary process and delivers—as a yeast in the dough of space and time—a new consciousness, a creative and compassionate Spirit. He inaugurates a dynamism of attraction and participation in the newness, in the wholeness of Love. In the light of Jesus' life we can glimpse and experience the disruptive, crucified, rising, and insurgent mystery emerged in the journey of the Universe.

How do we integrate death with grace—personally, communally, *planetarily* in our journey of faith? First of all, we can accept that time, trouble, vulnerability, grief, and death constitute the heartbeat of the world, together with the joyous promise of and our desire for a transformation and healing of the earth. Accepting that God is creating something new through time and death, suffering and struggle, especially in the global dark night of our age with regard to our political, economic, and financial structures that disintegrate communities, species, and environment. Spurred to take care for our common home, I feel that the present time is inviting each one of us—and all of us together—to embody feelings of wonder, compassion, and hope.[29] *Wonder* for the amazing blooming of life that has preceded us and appeals to our responsibility for the ongoing adventure of the cosmos. *Compassion* for the groaning planet earth that we are ravaging and that urges us to change our lifestyles. And *hope* that in the bottleneck we are living God will inspire in our hearts new capacities to favor the creativeness and novelty of the Spirit— unimaginable as that may be.

We conclude with a Lakota prayer:[30]

Aho Mitakuye Oyasin . . . All my relations. I honor you in this circle of life with me today. I am grateful for this opportunity to acknowledge you in this prayer . . .

To the Creator, for the ultimate gift of life, I thank you.

To the mineral nation that has built and maintained my bones and all foundations of life experience, I thank you.

To the plant nation that sustains my organs and body and gives me healing herbs for sickness, I thank you.

To the animal nation that feeds me from your own flesh and offers your loyal companionship in this walk of life, I thank you.

To the human nation that shares my path as a soul upon the sacred wheel of Earthly life, I thank you.

To the Spirit nation that guides me invisibly through the ups and downs of life and for carrying the torch of light through the Ages, I thank you.

To the Four Winds of Change and Growth, I thank you.

You are all my relations, my relatives, without whom I would not live. We are in the circle of life together, co-existing, co-dependent, co-creating our destiny. One, not more important than the other. One nation evolving from the other and yet each dependent upon the one above and the one below. All of us a part of the Great Mystery.

Thank you for this Life.

Notes

1. Saint Augustine, *On the Psalms*, Ancient Christian Writers series (New York: Newman, 1960), 272.

2. Christopher Fry, *A Sleep of Prisoners* (New York: Dramatists Play Service, 1953).

3. Joanna Macy and Molly Brown, *Coming Back to Life* (Stony Creek, CT: New Society, 2014).

4. Brian Thomas Swimme and Mary Evelyn Tucker, *Journey of the Universe* (New Haven, CT: Yale University Press, 2011), 99–100.

5. Cynthia Moe-Lobeda, *Resisting Structural Evil: Love as Ecological and Economic Vocation* (Minneapolis: Fortress, 2013).

6. Charles Eisenstein, *The Ascent of Humanity: Civilization and the Human Sense of Self* (Berkeley, CA: North Atlantic, 2013), 207.

7. Carolyn Baker, *Sacred Demise: Walking the Spiritual Path of Industrial Civilization's Collapse* (Bloomington, IN: iUniverse, 2009).

8. David Abram, *Becoming Animal: An Earthly Cosmology* (New York: Pantheon, 2010).

9. Julie Cadwallader Staub, "Measurement," *Spiritus* 13, no. 1 (Spring 2013): 120.

10. Joseph Campbell, *The Hero's Journey: Joseph Campbell on His Life and Work*, ed. Phil Cousineau (Novato, CA: New World Library, 2003), 10.

11. Neil Shubin, *The Universe Within: Discovering the Common History of Rocks, Planets, and People* (New York: Random House, 2013), ix–x.

12. Thomas Berry, "Twelve Principles for Understanding the Universe," in Thomas Berry, *Evening Thoughts: Reflecting on Earth as Sacred Community*, ed. Mary Evelyn Tucker, new edition (Berkeley, CA: Counterpoint, 2015), 145–47.

13. Elizabeth A. Johnson, *Ask the Beasts: Darwin and the God of Love* (London: Continuum, 2014), 144–53.

14. Kathleen Duffy, "Sophia: Catalyst for Creative Union and Divine Love," in *From Teilhard to Omega: Co-creating an Unfinished Universe*, ed. Ilia Delio (Maryknoll, NY: Orbis, 2014), 25.

15. Ilia Delio, *The Emergent Christ: Exploring the Meaning of Catholic in an Evolutionary Universe* (Maryknoll, NY: Orbis, 2011).

16. Barbara Deming, "Spirit of Love," in *We Are All Part of One Another: A Barbara Deming Reader*, ed. Jane Meyerding (Philadelphia: New Society, 1984).

17. Swimme and Tucker, *Journey of the Universe*, 90–91.

18. Jeremy Rifkin, *The Empathic Civilization: The Race to Global Consciousness in a World in Crisis* (New York: J.P. Tarcher/Penguin, 2009).

19. Michael Tomasello, *A Natural History of Human Thinking* (Cambridge, MA: Harvard University Press, 2014).

20. Ilia Delio, *The Emergent Christ*, 47.

21. John Haughey, *Where Is Knowing Going? The Horizons of the Knowing Subject* (Washington, DC: Georgetown University Press, 2009); Ilia Delio, *Making All Things New. Catholicism, Cosmology, Consciousness* (Maryknoll, NY: Orbis, 2015).

22. Rebecca del Rio, "Constant," quoted in Carolyn Baker, *Collapsing Consciously: Transformative Truths for Turbulent Times* (Berkeley, CA: North Atlantic, 2013), 172.

23. Johnson, *Ask the Beasts*, 182.

24. John F. Haught, *Making Sense of Evolution: Darwin, God, and the Drama of Life* (Louisville, KY: Westminster John Knox, 2010), 53.

25. Brian T. Swimme and Mary Evelyn Tucker, *Journey of the Universe: An Epic Story of Cosmic, Earth, and Human Transformation*, directed by Patsy Northcutt and David Kennard (Mill Valley, CA: Northcutt Productions, 2011), DVD.

26. Judy Cannato, *Radical Amazement: Contemplative Lessons from Black Holes, Supernovas, and Other Wonders of the Universe* (Notre Dame, IN: Sorin, 2006), 119–20.

27. Haught, *Making Sense of Evolution*, 53.

28. Ilia Delio, *The Unbearable Wholeness of Being: God, Evolution, and the Power of Love* (Maryknoll, NY: Orbis, 2013), 85.

29. See Pope Francis, *Laudato Si* (encyclical letter on Care for Our Common Home, May 24, 2015).

30. *Aho Mitakuye Oyasin*, http://www.pachamama.org/tag/mitakuye-oyasin.

Inspirational Sources

Baker, Carolyn. *Sacred Demise: Walking The Spiritual Path of Industrial Civilization's Collapse*. Bloomington, IN: iUniverse, 2009.

Berry, Thomas. *The Dream of the Earth*. San Francisco: Sierra Club Books, 1988.

———. *Evening Thoughts: Reflecting on Earth as Sacred Community*. New ed. Edited by Mary Evelyn Tucker. Berkeley, CA: Counterpoint, 2015.

———. *The Sacred Universe: Earth, Spirituality, and Religion in the Twenty-First Century*. New York: Columbia University Press, 2009.

Cannato, Judy. *Fields of Compassion: How the New Cosmology is Transforming Spiritual Life*. Notre Dame, IN: Sorin, 2010.

———. *Radical Amazement: Contemplative Lessons from Black Holes, Supernovas, and Other Wonders of the Universe*. Notre Dame, IN: Sorin, 2006.

Chaisson, Eric. *The Epic of Evolution: Seven Ages of the Cosmos*. New York: Columbia University Press, 2005.

Christian, David. *Maps of Time: An Introduction to Big History*. Berkeley: University of California Press, 2005.

Delio, Ilia. *The Emergent Christ: Exploring the Meaning of Catholic in an Evolutionary Universe*. Maryknoll, NY: Orbis, 2011.

———. *Making All Things New. Catholicity, Cosmology, Consciousness*. Maryknoll, NY: Orbis, 2015.

———. *The Unbearable Wholeness of Being: God, Evolution, and the Power of Love*. Maryknoll, NY: Orbis, 2013.

Duffy, Kathleen. "Sophia: Catalyst for Creative Union and Divine Love." In *From Teilhard to Omega: Co-creating an Unfinished Universe*, edited by Ilia Delio, 24–36. Maryknoll, NY: Orbis, 2014.

Francis, Pope. *Laudato Sì*. Encyclical letter on Care for Our Common Home. May 24, 2015. Online at: http://w2.vatican.va/content/francesco/en/encyclicals/documents/papa-francesco_20150524_enciclica-laudato-si.html.

Haught, John F. *God after Darwin: A Theology of Evolution*. Boulder, CO: Westview, 2008.

———. *Making Sense of Evolution: Darwin, God, and the Drama of Life*. Louisville, KY: Westminster John Knox, 2010.

———. *Resting on the Future: Catholic Theology for an Unfinished Universe*. NY: Bloomsbury Academic, 2015.

Johnson, Elizabeth A. *Ask the Beasts: Darwin and the God of Love*. London: Continuum, 2014.

———. *Quest for the Living God: Mapping Frontiers in the Theology of God*. New York: Continuum, 2011 (in particular, "Creator Spirit in the Evolving World," 181–201).

McFague, Sallie. *A New Climate for Theology: God, the World, and Global Warming*. Minneapolis: Fortress, 2008.

Needleman, Jacob. *An Unknown World: Notes on the Meaning of the Earth*. New York: Penguin, 2012.

Phipps, Carter. *Evolutionaries: Unlocking the Spiritual and Cultural Potential of Science's Greatest Idea*. New York: HarperCollins, 2012.

Rohr, Richard. *Immortal Diamond: The Search for Our True Self*. San Francisco: Jossey-Bass, 2013.

Spong, John Shelby. *Eternal Life: A New Vision*. New York: HarperCollins, 2009.

———. *The Fourth Gospel: Tales of a Jewish Mystic*. New York: HarperOne, 2014.

Schneiders, Sandra M. *Jesus Risen in Our Midst: Essays on the Resurrection of Jesus in the Fourth Gospel*. Collegeville, MN: Liturgical Press, 2013.

———. *The Resurrection: Did It Really Happen and Why Does That Matter?* Los Angeles: Marymount Institute Press, 2013.

Shubin, Neil. *The Universe Within: Discovering the Common History of Rocks, Planets, and People*. New York: Random House, 2013.

Swimme, Brian. *The Hidden Heart of the Cosmos: Humanity and the New Story*. Maryknoll, NY: Orbis, 1996.

———. *The Universe Is a Green Dragon: A Cosmic Creation Story*. Santa Fe, NM: Bear, 1985.

Swimme, Brian, and Thomas Berry. *The Universe Story: From the Primordial Flaring Forth to the Ecozoic Era*. San Francisco: HarperSan Francisco, 1992.

Swimme, Brian Thomas, and Mary Evelyn Tucker. *Journey of the Universe*. New Haven, CT: Yale University Press, 2011.

———. *Journey of the Universe: The Epic Story of Cosmic, Earth, and Human Transformation*. Directed by Patsy Northcutt and David Kennard. Mill Valley, CA: Northcutt Productions, 2011. DVD, 56 min.

Vaughan-Lee, Llewellyn, ed. *Spiritual Ecology: The Cry of the Earth*. Point Reyes, CA: The Golden Sufi Center, 2013.

Scripture Index

2 Corinthians	
5:17	101
13:11-13	28

Galatians	
3:26-29	100
5:16-25	55

Ephesians	
1:17-23	91
2:13-18	58
5:8-14	19

Philippians	
2:7	103
3:8-14	82

Colossians	
1:24-28	103

1 Thessalonians	
3:12–4:2	70

2 Thessalonians	
2:16–3:5	115

1 Timothy	
1:12-17	109

2 Timothy	
3:14–4:2	112

Hebrews	
1:1-6	4
7:23-28	67
12:1-4	106

James	
1:17-27	61
5:1-6	64

1 Peter	
1:8-12	97
2:4-9	25
3:18-22	44

1 John	
3:1-2	52
3:1-2, 21-24	73
4:8	17

Revelation	
5:11-14	88

Topical Index

Index of Names